The Archaeology of Institutional Confinement

The American Experience in Archaeological Perspective

UNIVERSITY PRESS OF FLORIDA

Florida A&M University, Tallahassee
Florida Atlantic University, Boca Raton
Florida Gulf Coast University, Ft. Myers
Florida International University, Miami
Florida State University, Tallahassee
New College of Florida, Sarasota
University of Central Florida, Orlando
University of Florida, Gainesville
University of North Florida, Jacksonville
University of South Florida, Tampa
University of West Florida, Pensacola

The American Experience in Archaeological Perspective
Edited by Michael S. Nassaney

The books in this series explore an event, process, setting, or institution that was significant in the formative experience of contemporary America. Each volume will frame the topic beyond an individual site and attempt to give the reader a flavor of the theoretical, methodological, and substantive issues that researchers face in their examination of that topic or theme. These books will be comprehensive overviews that will allow serious students and scholars to get a good sense of contemporary and past inquiries on a broad theme in American history and culture.

The Archaeology of Collective Action, by Dean J. Saitta (2007)
The Archaeology of Institutional Confinement, by Eleanor Conlin Casella (2007)

The Archaeology of Institutional Confinement

Eleanor Conlin Casella

Foreword by Michael S. Nassaney

University Press of Florida

Gainesville/Tallahassee/Tampa/Boca Raton

Pensacola/Orlando/Miami/Jacksonville/Ft. Myers/Sarasota

This research is funded by

 Arts & Humanities
Research Council

Library of Congress Cataloging-in-Publication Data
Casella, Eleanor Conlin.
The archaeology of institutional confinement / Eleanor Conlin Casella ;
foreword by Michael S. Nassaney.
p. cm.—(The American experience in archaeological perspective)
Includes bibliographical references and index.
ISBN 978-0-8130-3139-2 (alk. paper)
   1. Imprisonment—United States—History. 2. Prisons—United States—
History. 3. Social isolation—History. I. Title.
HV9466.C37 2007
365.'973—dc22   2007005246

The University Press of Florida is the scholarly publishing agency for the
State University System of Florida, comprising Florida A&M Univer-
sity, Florida Atlantic University, Florida Gulf Coast University, Florida
International University, Florida State University, New College of Florida,
University of Central Florida, University of Florida, University of North
Florida, University of South Florida, and University of West Florida.

University Press of Florida
15 Northwest 15th Street
Gainesville, FL 32611-2079
http://www.upf.com

To Leigh O'Regan,
for support, inspiration, and ten months in the sun.

*Happiness is
the mental
adjustment
to whatever
conditions
that surround
YOU*

—Anonymous cell graffiti,
U.S. Federal Penitentiary at Alcatraz Island

Contents

Figures

Tables

Foreword

The walls and barbed-wire fences that surround the Adult Correctional Institute along Interstate 95 are starkly visible to thousands of Rhode Island motorists even as they whiz by at seventy miles per hour. As a child returning from a day at the beach where we frolicked unfettered in the pounding surf, I often wondered as I glanced at this detention castle of stone and steel what it must have been like to inhabit that space, how one could escape, and if the staff who administered to the inmates weren't themselves also somehow imprisoned. The ACI, as it was known in the vernacular, was one of hundreds of social experiments established in the American landscape to segregate deviance from society.

An enduring challenge for a democratic society is to seek a balance between civil liberties and maintenance of the social order. Since the founding of the New Republic in the late eighteenth century, the need to confine, punish, rehabilitate, reform, and deter abnormal behavior has had a dramatic impact on the definition of American citizenship and the treatment of transgressions. There remains no clear consensus on the purpose of institutional confinement, its desired effects, or the conditions that can bring about conformity. In *The Archaeology of Institutional Confinement*, Eleanor Casella raises a central question: Why incarcerate? To provide a theoretical framework that informs scholarly examination of institutional life, Casella draws on current ideas from psychology, penology, criminology, history, anthropology, and archaeology. Clearly, power relations constitute the organizing principle for understanding our carceral culture as expressed in prisons, asylums, and detention camps as well as related settings like factories, hospitals, and schools where modes of discipline are inculcated. In this expanded Foucauldian world, analysis must encompass those in power as well as those whose lives are constrained by walls, fences, and bars. Casella shows that even under the most severe conditions individuals had some degree of agency or power to enact both a public and hidden transcript.

It is the materiality of those transcripts (and the structures against which they were forged) that make them amenable to fruitful archaeological investigation. The archaeology of prisons, penitentiaries, asylums, and relocation camps demonstrates how the material world was implicated in the carceral society and how archaeology contributes to a better understanding of the American experience.

To say that this is a timely study is an understatement. In the heat of the debate surrounding the Patriot Act, Abu Ghraib, and suspected terrorist detainees at Guantánamo Bay, the United States currently has the highest rate of institutional confinement in the world. According to the Department of Justice, 482 per 100,000 U.S. residents are subject to incarceration, which is approximately one in every 109 men and one in every 1,613 women. The United States now has over half the world's prisons, despite the fact that America has less than 5 percent of the world's population.

With these staggering statistics in mind, it would behoove us to investigate the successes and failures of the solutions that have been proposed for deviancy and nonconformity over the past two centuries. The roots of modern problems often lie buried immediately beneath our feet. The materiality of institutional confinement is readily accessible to archaeological research and the results can reveal as much about contemporary life as they do about the past. For example, excavated artifacts demonstrate how obsolete ceramics, frugal room furnishings, standardized uniforms, and limited medical supplies helped to cultivate a docile consciousness, while graffiti, tribal amulets, alcohol bottles, and bone dice represent challenges to the structures of power.

The premise of the American Experience in Archaeological Perspective series is that archaeologies of the recent past have a contribution to make to an anthropological understanding of the American experience. This series aims to highlight the results of such research and make it available to a wider audience. Considerable work has been conducted on post-Columbian archaeological sites in the United States since the 1960s. Federal legislation and the establishment of the Society for Historical Archaeology have encouraged the investigation of sites associated with all Americans, even those who have been marginalized, exiled, and denied the rights of citizenship. The result has been a broadened conception of our national heritage and a willingness to look into the darker recesses of our past. Historical archaeology is now poised to provide anthropological understandings of our nation's formative cultural and social institutions and to examine how that legacy can illuminate the path toward a more humanitarian future.

In the efforts to preserve and organize culture's clutter, historical archaeologists have located, identified, analyzed, and interpreted the detritus of countless events, processes, settings, and institutions that were significant in laying the foundations of contemporary America. Because that residue was not edited for content, it can inform the histories, cultures, and social identities of a broad cast of characters that were actively involved in the making of America. A critical reading of this material record brings into focus processes of conflict and cooperation, domination and resistance, struggle and accommodation—in Casella's words, "a story of power and endurance." These stories often contradict the officially sanctioned narratives that many of us were taught. By examining the American experience from an archaeological perspective we are afforded the opportunity to read between the lines of the documentary record to shed new light on the forces that shaped American thought and action at different historical moments.

Questions regarding our attitudes toward criminals, dependents, and the disenfranchised amount to unresolved grief that must be settled to allow for the honest, critical reflection needed for a progressive society. How can we understand the paradox of a country that celebrates liberty yet simultaneously incarcerates at an unprecedented rate? When has confinement succeeded in achieving its purpose? How do inmates cope with conditions of extreme material and psychological anxiety? Are we doomed to repeat past mistakes when driven by war hysteria that makes it psychologically easier to marginalize and criminalize threats to our national security, perceived or otherwise? How can archaeology help us to recover and resolve the grief that resulted from acts perpetrated upon our own people? Archaeology can be instrumental in commemorating important places that can serve as monuments to the American experience of institutional confinement. Sites like Japanese relocation camps or Alcatraz, for example, encourage a national dialogue over civil rights, citizenship, and the role of institutional confinement within modern American society.

Michael S. Nassaney
Series Editor

Preface and Acknowledgments

I grew up in San Francisco during the 1970s. Besides my recollections of free Shakespeare performances, loud rock concerts, and horrid stinging nettles in Golden Gate Park, I remember the ominous presence of an island in the Bay. Despite its recent closure, everyone knew it was a Bad Place, and for years I was frightened by the haunting wail of nocturnal fog horns, believing they warned of a dangerous escape from the menacing rock. Two decades later, I finally visited Alcatraz with my Mum and Gran. By then a National Park, the island provided a discordant experience of sea spray, sunshine, discipline, and gloom. I could see my distant university Campanile across the bay. My Gran remarked that the sea lions were able to swim the distance between Alcatraz Island and Berkeley. Why couldn't the inmates?

This volume has grown out of my fascination with the ubiquitous phenomena of confinement. While I firmly believe that the modern state retains a basic duty to ensure the protection of its citizens from vicious, predatory, or desperate behaviors, I also wonder if institutional confinement has provided a panacea—a necessary response and cure for these crimes. Or whether these horrible places merely serve as temporary (and tremendously expensive) means for isolating those who engage in antisocial activities. Now living outside the United States, I am ashamed by the recent extension of a particularly hostile version of institutional confinement to a group of men who may (or may not) have threatened the American state. I wonder if the threat of terrorism—or simple fear itself—is enough to encourage my fellow Americans toward the abandonment of internationally recognized civil rights or the refusal of basic human dignity. Where did such institutions originate? How were people treated within these places? What does this experience produce? Why bother with incarceration? Considering the diverse historical, theoretical, and archaeological perspectives on this unique mode of population management, what is the underlying purpose of institutional confinement?

A number of individuals and organizations have supported my work on this project and therefore deserve sincere gratitude and recognition. Robert Paynter suggested my original involvement in this series, and Michael Nassaney provided essential editorial assistance and encouragement throughout the writing process. Eli Bortz, my editor at the University Press of Florida, offered enthusiastic guidance throughout the final stages of production. Elizabeth Peña,

Suzanne Spencer-Wood, Sherene Baugher, David Bush, Owen Lindauer, Susan Wurtzburg, Leo Barker, Martin Mayer, Jeff Burton, and particularly LuAnne De Cunzo offered essential graphic resources and editorial perspectives. Susan Ewing-Haley, park archivist from the Golden Gate National Parks and Recreational Area (NPS), Glen Rice from the Arizona State University Office of Cultural Resource Development, and Dan Mitchell from the Special Collections Library at University College London offered valued assistance with archival access and image reproduction permissions. Joy Oakley brought me to Rye for high tea and a bit of castle photography on a chilly December afternoon.

This project was made possible through a teaching relief grant from the Arts and Humanities Research Council of Britain. Further, I would like to specially acknowledge Richard Waterhouse and the School of Philosophical and Social Enquiry at the University of Sydney, Australia, for offering essential support during the writing stage of this manuscript. My colleagues there—Allison Betts, Dan Potts, Martin Gibbs, and Annie Clarke—all provided intellectual inspiration, logistic support, and a very generous welcome during my wonderful months Down Under. Special recognition is due Vanessa Hardy, Kylie Seretis, Darren Griffin, and Denis Gojak for IT support and social sustenance. My Father has offered generous advice and logistic assistance, typically during pivotal moments in the production of this manuscript. Finally, I would like to thank my Mum, both for helping me conquer my fear of Alcatraz Island so many years ago and subsequently for funding my image reproduction debts to the Golden Gate National Recreational Area archive office.

1

The Carceral Society

I continue to sleep in my allotted cell, and I wear the same clothing and eat the same breakfast, in silence if you can call it silence, forty women, most of them in here for nothing worse than stealing, who sit chewing their bread with their mouths open and slurping their tea in order to make a noise of some sort even if not speech, with an edifying Bible passage read out loud. You can have your own thoughts then, but if you laugh you must pretend you are coughing or choking . . .

—Margaret Atwood, *Alias Grace*

During November 2004, more than 1.5 million Americans were incarcerated within prisons, jails, and correctional facilities (Russell 2004). With one out of every 142 American residents institutionally confined, these statistics represented not only the largest prison population in the world, but also the highest number of inmates as a proportion of the total national population. Already, by December 2001, over $24 billion was spent annually across America to confine an estimated 1.2 million nonviolent criminals (Schiraldi 2002). But the evolution of this carceral society was neither inevitable nor accidental. This volume explores the origins and development of American institutional confinement as a unique, historical, and peculiarly modern phenomenon.

Why confine members of American society? Who becomes subjected to confinement, and under what circumstances? How do people experience confinement? What material conditions characterize institutional life? How did early communal forms of social welfare and punishment transform into the stark penitentiaries and fortified compounds of the twentieth century? What explains the paradox of a country that celebrates itself as a beacon of individual liberty, yet simultaneously incarcerates on a scale matched only by the Russian Federation (Walmsley 2001; see also Parenti 1999 and Christianson 1998)? Drawing from historical, theoretical, and archaeological perspectives, this study considers the rise of institutional confinement as a specific mode of population management. It traces the phenomenon from its historical and theoretical origins in late medieval Europe to its ubiquitous and controversial presence within contemporary America.

Lockdown: Confinement and the Exercise of Social Power

And all these gates, it develops a much stronger psychological outlook that you must control yourself. In a sense it brings static, it brings hate. You see all these bars, it's like locking you off from the rest of the world. There's a big 40-foot wall out there, all over the institution. And you have to come through the wall to come in, right? Who's going over the wall?

—Hans Toch, *Living in Prison*, inmate interview

In his influential sociological account of community dynamics within the New Jersey State Prison at Trenton, Gresham Sykes characterized incarceration as a painful experience of deprivation—a loss of the psychological, environmental, and material means for self-preservation. Further, as inmates struggled to individually and collectively soothe this arduous state of forfeiture, a distinctive "Society of Captives" (Sykes 1958) emerged to choreograph the internal power relations of the institution. Archaeological studies of institutional sites have, often unwittingly, illuminated aspects of Sykes' classic sociological model—providing material evidence of both the nature and extent of formal privations and alleviation practices that distinguish places of confinement.

While the binary structure of Sykes' model has been extensively refined over subsequent decades, underlying elements of his study can be found throughout all institutional forms. Places of confinement—whether workhouses, asylums, prison camps, relocation centers, industrial schools, or penitentiaries—essentially exist to enforce a deprivation of liberty. To varying degrees, institutional life can be characterized by a loss of autonomy, material possessions, individual expression, community and family life, and even basic personal security. Further, institutions reflect the diverse coping strategies undertaken by those confined to ameliorate some measure of this incessant distress. Therefore, as demonstrated throughout this volume, social power serves as the central dynamic of institutional confinement. Whether defined as an oppositional relationship of domination and resistance, as an embodied engagement with institutional regulations and rituals, or as a subversive means for minimizing the everyday pains of confinement, social power infuses the modern institution.

Archaeological studies of institutional sites have offered both functionalist and experiential perspectives to these broader scholarly understandings of social power. Drawing upon a diverse range of artifactual, documentary, cartographic, and architectural sources, archaeologists have forged a richly detailed knowledge of the specific material conditions of power that structure places of confinement. Archaeology has demonstrated how power operated, or functioned, upon institutional inhabitants. It has interpreted the physical remains of perimeter stockades, room partitions, monotonous site layouts, workshop facilities, metal-alloy whistles, industrial machinery, obsolete ceramic assemblages, uniforms, and food remains to reveal how power was materially exerted over those confined. Equally, archaeology has demonstrated how inhabitants co-opted their surrounding material world to retain some measure of control. This research has revealed how graffiti, personal possessions, escape tunnels, ethnic foodways, gaming tokens, and alcohol bottles—the subversive material culture inevitably recovered from institutional sites—produced an effective challenge to the power relations of confinement.

Recent archaeological studies have also provided more experiential perspectives on the nature of social power. By interrogating the material world of institutions as a constellation of lived practices, archaeologists have illuminated the diverse embodied experiences of everyday institutional life. This work has demonstrated how material aspects of living conditions—evidence including skeletal malformations, glass assemblages dominated by medicinal supplies, architectural responses to adverse climates, symbolic gardens and drawing rooms, hygienic instruction and drills, regulated daily schedules of exercise and isolation, muster yards, and repetitive labor practices—all generated a distinctive understanding or "consciousness" of hierarchical social relations specific to those confined. In this phenomenological approach, the physical bodies and material encounters of institutional inhabitants are seen to reflect, or "map," broader patterns of power in American society.

Ultimately, popular justifications for institutional confinement raise deeper questions of social power. Why does a state imprison members of its citizenry? Many scholars have perceived confinement as a form of punishment or "the infliction of hard treatment by an authority on a person for his prior failing in some respect (usually an infraction of a rule or command)" (Feinberg 1972: 25). Others have observed a rehabilitative purpose, explaining confinement as a disciplinary mechanism for transforming dangerous or dependent individuals into self-sufficient and reintegrated citizens (Foucault 2001 [1964]; Tonry and Petersilia 2000). With prison populations of Western nations increasing exponentially over the late twentieth century, a more cynical perspective has begun to prevail. Confinement has become identified as a means of socioeconomic neutralization—of human warehousing (Parenti 1999; Mathiesen 1990; Rafter 1990; Katz 1986; Ignatieff 1978). The concept of social power is threaded throughout these various justifications. Whether perceived as a force of retribution, reformation, or segregation, the authoritative exertion of state power has been inevitably summoned to explain the endurance of this uniquely modern form of population management.

On Industry, Order, and Citizenship

With the rise of industrial capitalism from the late eighteenth century, questions of productivity have also framed the delineation of "citizens" from "noncitizens." The experience of institutional confinement was originally intended as a mechanism of social transformation, a means for changing those who did not (or could not) work into laboring citizens. But despite these grand designs, institutional confinement failed its symbiotic relationship with modern capitalism. As demonstrated through the archaeological studies of this volume, institutionally mobilized forms of unfree labor remained costly, limited in scope, and ultimately noncompetitive. Why then do we find the stubborn endurance, if not enthusiastic expansion, of this prohibitively expensive mode of population management over the last three centuries?

A study of institutional confinement immediately begs questions of citizenship, civil rights, and social defense. These complex topics have flavored broader debates over national identity from the heady optimistic decades of the New Republic through the insecure years of the early twenty-first century. Although founded on humanistic ideologies of freedom and democracy, America has paradoxically adopted institutional confinement with a special enthusiasm. Why did this passion emerge? Certainly, a modern state retains basic duties to punish vicious and antisocial behaviors, to protect its law-abiding citizens from internal threats and social decay. However, for a society to thrive, a delicate equilibrium must be sustained between protection of the social order and protection of individual civil rights. By examining the materiality of institutional life, we can interrogate the shifting nature of that balance over the last three centuries. From the seventeenth century onwards, how did places of confinement operate to neutralize, or in some cases transform, threats to American society? How did they provide essential public support for the vulnerable, criminal, and disenfranchised? And most importantly, what would the dominance of institutional confinement reveal about the intrinsic structures and underlying integrity of American society?

By Way of Synopsis

Given the vast diversity of literature on institutional confinement, the chapters of this volume focus on three interdisciplinary approaches to understanding this modern phenomenon. Chapter 2 examines the historical evolution of American institutions. Starting in the post-Reformation era of early modern Europe, this story begins with "The Great Confinement" of the mid-seventeenth century (Foucault 2001 [1964]) as new monumental and multifunctional institutions were established to provide punishment, alms, and medical relief to the dangerous and desperate of European urban centers. With profound socioeconomic and philosophical differences distinguishing English from continental modes of social welfare, material differences in the earliest institutions of the American colonial era may have served as an archaeological reflection of these two disparate approaches to public charity. By the optimistic decades of the New Republic, ideologies of citizenship, liberty, and opportunity influenced American institutional philosophy. Confinement became envisioned as an opportunity for social and personal transformation, as a humane alternative to the sanguinary punishments of Old Europe, and as a means for regulating the disbursement of public poor relief funds. As British models for "reformed" institutions diffused across the Atlantic, America warmly embraced new disciplinary designs for workhouses and penitentiaries. From the 1830s, enthusiastic debates over competing institutional systems raged among civic leaders and welfare activists. The rapid proliferation of austere, monumental institutions across the nation marked the subsequent three decades as the golden age of American confinement.

Such intoxicating optimism was soon to evaporate. With the advent of the American Civil War, confinement provided a new method of internal exile. Captured soldiers from both Union and Confederate armies filled POW camps, and the institution emerged as a means for "warehousing" ambiguously defined "noncitizens." Over the second half of the nineteenth century, institutional confinement extended to an increasingly diverse population of Americans, with private leasing schemes applied to the disproportionately African-American populations of Southern penitentiaries and industrial boarding schools established to cultivate the assimilation of Native American children across the American West. With the turn-of-century Progressive Era, the U.S. federal government adopted institutional confinement as a centralized state power, a shift first marked by the creation of the Federal Prison System in 1891 and dramatically extended during the relocation and confinement of Japanese-Americans during World War II. To consider how these complex issues articulate today, this chapter concludes with a brief consideration of current debates over citizenship, civil rights, confinement, public protection, and state power as America enters the twenty-first century.

Chapter 3 offers an interdisciplinary range of theoretical perspectives on institutional confinement, demonstrating how different understandings of power shape each ideological position. Starting with classic criminological approaches, this chapter first explores retribution, deterrence, and reform as the traditionally recognized aims of incarceration. These socioeconomic models contrast with the sociological, anthropological, legal, and historical approaches that have coalesced into the multidisciplinary field of penality studies. Concerned with the production of social control, this second theoretical school is characterized by a functionalist focus on the internal dynamics of carceral discipline. Defining the institutional experience as a perpetual relationship between forces of domination and resistance, penality scholars have revealed both the techniques by which confinement produces voluntary compliance and the strategies by which inmates cope within the disciplinary environment.

Chapter 3 then turns to recent feminist, poststructuralist, and postcolonial critiques of the binary dualism that inherently frames penality studies. Perceiving institutionalization as an embodied experience, scholars within this third approach have explored diverse and multiple forms of subjectivity created under confinement. By exposing the ritualistic, transformational, and experiential aspects of institutional life, these perspectives have interrogated the wider dynamics of class, gender, and race that proliferate within modern institutions. Finally, to provide a platform for new material perspectives, the chapter's fourth section examines the strategic negotiations and situational mobilizations of power that structure everyday institutional life. Anthropological models of indigenous gift exchange are integrated with sociological studies of "inmate subcultures" to consider incarceration as a perpetual relation of exchange between (un)willing participants. Exploring concepts of "reciprocity," this final group of scholars seeks to understand how institutional occupants opportunistically mobilize their social, material, and sexual relationships to minimize their disadvantages and ultimately survive confinement.

Drawing upon these historical and theoretical perspectives, chapter 4 presents the material experience of American institutional confinement through a series of archaeological case studies. These projects have examined the cultural landscapes, built environments, and artifactual assemblages from three distinct modes of American confinement: prisons, workhouses, and places of exile. By contrasting these institutional types, chapter 4 considers how the underlying *purpose* of these institutions became reflected in broader patterns of unfree labor and living conditions, of discipline and insubordination, of austerity and survival.

Finally, chapter 5 briefly considers what material perspectives have contributed to our understandings of the modern institution. First, archaeological research has examined the range of living conditions supported within places of confinement. Evidence drawn from skeletal, faunal, and artifactual sources has demonstrated the nature and quality of material resources provided for various types of institutional inhabitants—inmates, residents, detainees, administrators, and supervisory staff. Further, archaeological studies have illuminated the central role of unfree labor in the establishment, maintenance, and justification of institutional sites. Organized as both subsidized and privatized forms of labor, these operations have ranged from skilled craft production and vocational training programs to manual construction works and congregate industrial production. Case studies reveal the nature of this unfree labor through both the institutional architecture and the physical residue of the tasks themselves—the machinery, tools, raw materials, debitage, rejects, and finished commodities.

Third, archaeology has rigorously engaged broader scholarly debates by interpreting the everyday materiality of institutional life as a physical expression of social power. These studies have not only detailed how and why the institutional fabric has actively forged a coercive environment upon the inhabitants, but also how the occupants have refashioned their material worlds to support alternative relations of coping, insubordination, compromise, exchange, and survival. Finally, archaeology has provided an important temporal perspective on the care and treatment of those disenfranchised from American society. By exploring the nature of institutional life over the recent past, these studies have illuminated changing patterns of confinement from the early colonial workhouses of the seventeenth century through the austere penitentiaries of the twentieth century.

Does institutional confinement "mark a special and exclusionary relationship" between a state and its citizenry (Wacquant 2001: 106)? Does it represent an imperfect yet necessary technology for protecting the lives, property, and opportunities of law-abiding citizens (Tonry and Petersilia 2000; N. Morris 1998)? Does it provide a place of "supervised liberty" (Pratt 2002) for those who do not (or cannot) fit within the norms of mainstream society? Or does the modern institution merely operate as a "big lockup," a place "to terrorize the poor, warehouse social dynamite and social wreckage, and . . . reproduce apolitical forms of criminal 'deviance'" (Parenti 1999: 169). By appreciating the unique materiality of punishment, welfare support, and social exclusion during the recent past, we can consider the complex ambiguities between these positions. We can begin to understand the pivotal role of institutional confinement within the American experience.

2

The Gentle Apparatus

A Historical Overview of Institutional Confinement

The origins of American institutional confinement began not in the New World colonies, but rather in Europe. By the end of the sixteenth century, dissolution of Catholic religious orders had effectively destabilized pre-Reformation modes of care for the socially vulnerable. Over the next century, traditional monastic, religious, manorial, and parish-based establishments became increasingly replaced by experimental institutions organized according to Enlightenment philosophies of order and reason (Huey 2001; Spierenburg 1998; Hirsch 1992: 13–31). As discussed in chapter 1, the goal of these new places of detention was not merely to collect and confine those who introduced disorder into society, but to enact a radical program of "re-formation" on those who had become disfigured by their particular social pathology—whether infirmity, poverty, treason, or criminality. Designed in accordance with Protestant ideologies of virtuous labor and self-improvement, the new asylums were intended to provide a "cure" for such social malformations, converting habits of idleness into habits of industry. Thus, in this post-Reformation world of emerging mercantile capitalism, institutions first appeared as places of transformation and progress, where the socially vulnerable could be rehabilitated (by coercion if necessary) into respectable, hard-working, and economically productive subjects of the crown.

The Great Confinement: Birth of "The Institution" in Early Modern Europe

During the early decades of the seventeenth century, as permanent colonies were founded in North America, the first institutions of confinement were established throughout England and continental Europe to channel the poor, landless, and unemployed into productive forms of labor. While their origins could be traced to the medieval "hospitals" run by religious orders throughout Europe, early seventeenth-century almshouses revealed a new protoinstitutional form through their distinctive organization of space (Heath 1910).

Like the monastic cloister (Gilchrist 1994), the hospital of the Middle Ages emphasized communal movement between interior spaces. Shared residential accommodation was arranged along a long, dormitory hall with multiple points of access, often with a chapel situated at one end. Additional communal space, in the form of courtyards, terraces, or dining rooms, was also a common feature. Other late medieval almshouses, including an early sixteenth-century English example in Glastonbury Abbey, Somerset (Ponsford 1994), were established as part of an existing Roman Catholic monastery. In these examples, specific rooms in the cloister were dedicated to charitable relief, where the parish homeless could seek accommodation after receiving donations of food, clothing, or money at the gate of the monastery.

In contrast, protoinstitutional almshouses of the sixteenth century were organized around principles of segregation and restricted access, the internal accommodation designed as single-unit "tenements" with separate entrances and communal spaces comparatively limited in both size and function. From the late sixteenth century, almshouses in many English villages were constructed as single-story rows of connected dwellings designed for the segregation of occupants into living units. These early structures formed the oldest example of terraced housing in Europe (Huey 2001: 132). Practices of surveillance and ordered symmetry began to emerge from late seventeenth-century Restoration-era architectural layouts, with larger English urban almshouses designed as rectilinear quadrangles around open courtyards as in Colston's Almshouse, Bristol (1691). These examples of early protoinstitutional design also emphasized a closer scrutiny of access and movement, with the main entrance gate frequently flanked by rooms provided for the chaplain, warden, or in the case of Morden College, Blackheath (1685), the almshouse treasurer (Markus 1993: 97).

By 1647, Parliament appointed the London Corporation of the Poor to oversee the erection of the London Workhouse, one of the first urban structures architecturally fabricated for the sole and explicit purpose of institutional confinement (Markus 1993: 98). Most significantly, its architectural design included an early attempt to structurally distinguish and separate types of occupants. The building was originally constructed with a central chapel connecting separate wings for destitute children and petty criminals. However, this early example of institutional design proved to be well ahead of its time, as the block fell quickly into disuse and was eventually demolished. Thus, while British government statutes throughout the seventeenth and eighteenth centuries increasingly codified and refined specific types of activities requiring confinement, in practice the ambiguous intermingling of designs intended for employment, social care, and punishment emerged as a characteristic feature of carceral institutions. By the end of the seventeenth century, the workhouse had become the first European type of carceral institution for social management.

Continental Europe had witnessed a similar development of early protoinstitutional forms by the end of the sixteenth century (Spierenburg 1998: 61–65). In the Netherlands, establishment of the first male house of correction occurred in 1589. By the beginning of the seventeenth century the facility was known as the Rasphuis or Saw House, where destitute men rasped (pulverized) logs of wood into a powder locally valued as a textile dye. A similar Spinhuis was established for women during 1596, again named for the type of employment undertaken within (Huey 2001: 125). By the seventeenth century, these types of establishments for public assistance evolved into more formal, architecturally designed institutions. Enlarged in 1604, the Old Men's House in Amsterdam consisted of an impressive central structure with flanking dormitory bays arranged in a rectilinear layout around formal courtyard gardens. In the twenty years after 1640, almshouses, workhouses, and institutions for orphans, widows, and elderly women were established in Amsterdam. By 1681, the monumental Old Women's House was constructed along the Amstel River, its thirty-one bays providing "the broadest frontage of any building in Amsterdam" (Huey 2001: 126–27).

In his classic study of institutionalization, Michel Foucault (2001 [1964]) declared the foundation of L'Hôpital Général in Paris during 1656 as the birth of "the Great Confinement." Established under royal edict by Louis XIV, this infamous and monumental institution consisted of several affiliated infirmary facilities and jails. Explicitly designed as a catchall place of confinement for those members of French society deemed unproductive and "unreasonable," the General Hospital accommodated a colorful mix from the fringes of society, including beggars, debtors, prisoners, invalids, orphans, prostitutes, blasphemers, the elderly, and the insane (Markus 1993). To exact rehabilitation, inmates were compelled to labor "as both a remedy to unemployment and a stimulus to the development of manufactories" (Foucault 2001 [1964]: 49). Each Parisian trade guild was required to provide two journeymen for training purposes. Provisions for punishment of recalcitrance were provided by royal edict in the form of whipping posts, iron collars, prisons, and dungeons. The General Hospital thus assumed a new ethical status:

> the Hôpital does not have the appearance of a mere refuge for those whom age, infirmity, or sickness keep from working; it will have not only the aspect of a forced labor camp, but also that of a moral institution responsible for punishing, for correcting a certain moral "abeyance" which does not merit the tribunal of men, but cannot be corrected by the severity of penance alone. (Foucault 2001 [1964]: 55)

It was this moral charge combined with the state-granted authority for repressive control that had become the unique hallmark of institutional confinement by the beginning of the eighteenth century. Other European states duplicated these grand provisions, with the Ospizio Generale established by Pope Innocent XI in 1686 to confine the poor of Rome and the octagonally segregated Maison de Force designed for Vicomte Jean Jacques Philippe Vilain XIII in Ghent by 1722 (Spierenburg 1998: 61; Markus 1993: 121; Evans 1982: 68).

As few formal, specialized institutions existed in colonial America, confinement emerged as only one out of a wider range of methods for dealing with the unproductive, undesired, and socially vulnerable. During the colonial period, local jails primarily detained law breakers on remand—in other words, during preparations for their trial date. Punishment for crimes and habitual debt involved either the imposition of fines or public corporeal chastisements, such as the stocks, whipping, branding, exile, or execution (Hirsch 1992: 3–8).

Paupers were either auctioned off to local farmers as subsidized laborers or supported through some form of "outdoor relief" (Spencer-Wood and Baugher 2001: 5–8). This latter method of social welfare involved direct support given to maintain the poor, mentally ill, elderly, widowed, orphaned, and injured in their own households and communities. Funds for outdoor relief were raised locally through a combination of municipal taxation and humanitarian donations from church and private philanthropic sources (Katz 1986). Alms granted through outdoor relief tended to consist of either small amounts of cash or relief in kind, such as food, clothing, and winter fuel. In contrast to later institutional forms of poverty management, outdoor relief did not involve the provision of accommodation or periods of enforced labor.

Finally, those considered dangerous or undesirable strangers—primarily Native Americans or people identified as "rogues" or "vagabonds"—were simply exiled from colonial territories (Rothman 1990: 5). Such distinctions served to socially differentiate between residents and nonresidents, colonists and outsiders. Thus, pre-Revolutionary modes of social management tended to rely on existing traditional forms of social control that emphasized the presence or absence of local kinship ties and on community obligations for support, punishment, and reform.

Asylums for the Poor: From Almshouse to Workhouse in the American Colonies

As outposts of empire, the American colonies naturally developed methods of poor relief management modeled on the laws and traditions of Europe. Replicating English and continental modes of confinement (Markus 1993: 99; Driver 1993), early American institutions were primarily divided into those established for the "deserving" versus the "undeserving" poor. Thus, while the sick, infirm, elderly, and insane were accommodated in almshouses or asylums, the able-bodied poor were considered idle mendicants and incarcerated within houses of correction, houses of industry, bridewells, workhouses, and town farms.

Comparing the origins of almshouses in the Dutch and English colonies of North America, Paul Huey (2001) reveals a fundamental cultural difference behind their financial support mechanisms for poor relief. This variation reflects contrasting European philosophies of socioeconomic responsibility and obligation in the wake of the Protestant Reformation. In England, the dissolution of monasteries in 1534 led to the royal confiscation of all property of the Roman Catholic Church. Major ecclesiastical sites were thus transferred to the newly established Church of England, presided over by the English monarch. Under the terms of the Elizabethan Poor Law of 1575 (officially identified as 43 Elizabeth), responsibility for poor relief fell to frequently impoverished local parish (township) authorities. In the relatively wealthy urban districts of London, Bristol, and Nottingham a limited number of private and guild-sponsored workhouses became established for both accommodation and punishment purposes. The absence of traditional religious forms of poor relief caused private charitable donations to increase. On both sides of the Atlantic, the new wealth and status enjoyed by the emerging English bourgeois urban classes of merchants and tradesmen became displayed through charitable bequests and donations for the establishment and support of poorhouses (Berridge 1987; Katz 1986: 10–15). Thus, in the English colonies of North America, such as Pennsylvania, Rhode Island, Connecticut, and Massachusetts, private philanthropy quickly became the dominant form of financial support for both almshouses and workhouses.

In contrast, seizure of former Catholic Church property in the Netherlands resulted in its transfer to local magistrates. These local authorities subsequently reapportioned the confiscated resources among towns, charitable foundations, and Protestant churches. Traditional Dutch concepts of charity emphasized the activity as a public duty, conferring prestige, dignity, and citizenship upon the successful merchant who disbursed part of his wealth in charitable public projects. The paternalism informing this model carried over into charitable administration. Unofficial titles of workhouse staff emphasized a paternal identity, with the head of staff frequently known as the "indoor father" or "food father" and his wife as the "food mother" (Spierenburg 1998: 62). As noted by the social historian Simon Schama, "At the centre of the Dutch world was a burgher, not a bourgeois. . . . [The] burgher was a citizen first and a *homo oeconomicus* second. And the obligations of civism conditioned the opportunities of prosperity" (1987: 7).

Both before and after the Reformation, alms were collected from church congregations and distributed and administered by the clergy (Peña 2001: 156). As a result, the 1640 colonial charter for establishment of the Dutch Reform Church in New Amsterdam (later New York) certified its obligation and responsibility for poor relief (Ross 1988: 140). Over the next twenty-five years of Dutch colonial presence in North America, the Reform Church held the primary role in both the distribution of public assistance funds and the establishment and administration of institutions, including the church-owned almshouses of Albany (ca. 1652) and New York (1655). Even with the acquisition of the New Netherland colony by England in 1664, privatization of poor relief and asylums was not widely accepted. The Dutch Reform Church maintained its authority over poverty management into the eighteenth century.

These profoundly divergent European approaches to poor relief may have in turn produced the differences apparent in comparative patterns of relief activity in the American colonies. For example, Huey's documentary study (2001) identifies remarkably low levels of charitable bequests made by New Yorkers during the late seventeenth century, with donations included in 5.9 percent of wills in Ulster County, New York, as compared to 14.3 percent in Suffolk County, Massachusetts (135, 142). Although he correlates these charity rates with differences in "the severity of the poor relief problem" (149), his results may also demonstrate an underlying tradition of privatization in the English-founded colony of Massachusetts. Conversely, the relatively better diet and middle-class tablewares recovered from excavation of the eighteenth-century New York City Almshouse (presented as a detailed case study in chapter 4) may represent a residual consequence of the publicly oriented "economic philosophy" of charity in the former Dutch colony (Baugher 2001: 198–99).

Despite these underlying differences in the nature of poor relief, by the mid-eighteenth century, secular institutions had been established throughout the colonies to accommodate and reform the growing numbers of destitute. As a particularly expensive response to a widespread social problem, institutional confinement was at first concentrated in the larger towns and cities of colonial America, with poorhouses established in Boston (1664), Salem, Massachusetts (1719), Portsmouth, New Hampshire (1716), Newport, Rhode Island (1723), Philadelphia (1732), New York City (1736), Charlestown, South Carolina (1736), Providence, Rhode Island (1753), and Baltimore, Maryland (1773) (Katz 1986: 14).

Archaeological studies of eighteenth-century American almshouses of the colonial and post-Revolutionary periods have demonstrated that the majority followed a common plan adopted from the earlier European models. Like the grand public institutions of Amsterdam, Bristol, and London, American almshouses tended to follow a rectilinear design, with a primary or administrative building flanked by support buildings all arranged around a square open courtyard. In the New York City Almshouse complex (1736), outbuildings added to the compound over a sixty-year period included a kitchen, hospital, wash house, stables, and a storehouse (Baugher and Lenik 1997: 10). Similarly, a poorhouse constructed in the rural tidewater parish of Stratton Major, Virginia (1772), included a main structure of 36 by 16 feet, a cornhouse, and a henhouse arranged around a shared garden (McCartney 1987: 295). In both of these examples, the designs followed European counterparts in the elaboration of the compound with additional *separate* structures, rather than with additions to the original almshouse structure. In contrast, the Philadelphia house of employment and almshouse (1767), although arranged in a three-sided rectilinear layout around a central courtyard, included separate wings for the "industrious" and "vicious" poor contained within a single, continuous building (De Cunzo 1995: 14).

Many scholars have questioned the nature and quality of life within these early institutions. In his historical study of American asylums (1990), David Rothman characterized eighteenth-century forms of respite care as patterned upon "family" structures, both in terms of their external appearance and internal arrangements (42–43). Located within town boundaries, the typical almshouse lacked distinctive institutional architecture. As chapter 4 will discuss, many counties saved on construction costs by purchasing an available private residence or farmhouse and using the existing structure with minimal modifications (Strauss and Spencer-Wood 1999; De Cunzo 1995). Rothman further suggests that daily routines and arrangements of accommodation mirrored that of the ordinary working class, causing the asylum to operate like a large extended household rather than a disciplinary institution. In contrast, other historians offer a much harsher image of early municipal respite care, emphasizing the "intolerable and mean-spirited" organization of daily life within the almshouses (Ross 1988: 156). According to this alternative perspective, the workhouse was explicitly established to dissuade long-term dependency by providing a strict and abstinent lifestyle "so undesirable that any life outside, except in extreme circumstances, would be preferable" (Markus 1993: 141; see also Driver 1993).

Archaeological studies have found evidence for both experiences of institutional confinement during the antebellum period. In her study of the Magdalen Society of Philadelphia (1995), Lu Ann De Cunzo demonstrates the purposeful selection of a residential garden suburb for the location of the society's first asylum for "fallen women" in 1807 (38–39). The reconstruction of their asylum buildings in the 1840s allowed the society to adopt a bourgeois neoclassical style of architecture, including residential amenities such as indoor plumbing and central heating. The display of such domestic architecture was undertaken to mark a stark ideological and gendered contrast with the disciplinary designs adopted for contemporary Philadelphian penal institutions for men at Walnut Street and Cherry Hill. Similarly, Sherene Baugher's archaeological study of the eighteenth-century municipal almshouse in New York City (2001) indicates a notable difference in conditions experienced by those considered deserving poor one hand and undeserving poor on the other. Noting that the compassionate household atmosphere of the city's almshouse may not have extended into to the adjacent "bridewell" workhouse, Baugher argues that the quality of life under early American forms of institutional confinement probably lay somewhere between Rothman's ideal household and Ross' austere institution (197–99).

Archaeological assemblages recovered from colonial-era almshouses indicate a frugal, but not restrictively meager, lifestyle. As chapter 4 will bear out in more detail, the variety of decorated ceramic tablewares—including tin-glazed earthenwares (delft), Chinese import porcelains, hand-painted pearlwares, and transfer-printed creamwares—recovered during excavations of eighteenth-century almshouse complexes in both New York City and Albany appears to represent frequent practices of charitable contribution by affluent members of colonial society (Baugher 2001; Huey 2001). Although such practices could reflect obligations of civism particular to the Dutch origins of these settlements, other examples of early nineteenth-century almshouses established in the former English colonies have suggested similar patterns of charitable donation in ceramics and glass tablewares (Strauss and Spencer-Wood 1999; Garman and Russo 1999; De Cunzo 1995). Results from analysis of excavated faunal materials indicate that inmates of New York–based almshouses had access to a modest yet varied diet and benefited from both municipally confiscated foods and charitable donations (Baugher 2001). Although archaeological research on almshouses has only recently begun to develop new comparative perspectives on the nature of class and gender relations, the material and archival evidence itself has provided significant insight into the nature of daily life experienced by the poor, infirm, and out-of-luck in American society from the colonial era through the first decades of the New Republic.

A Palace for Felons: The Origins of Modern Penal Incarceration

Over the eighteenth century, a second mode of American institutional confinement—criminal management—evolved in parallel with the almshouse. To consider the colonial origins of the modern penitentiary, we must again return to Europe. Before the late eighteenth century, traditional systems of punishment on both sides of the Atlantic relied heavily on public rituals of humiliation and corporeal chastisement, such as banishment, whipping, branding, and hanging. Use of the latter reached its apotheosis under the Bloody Code, a series of English laws enacted between 1688 and 1765 that required capital punishment for no less than 225 offenses (Ignatieff 1978: 16). Emerging from the Monetary Revolution of the 1690s, the vast majority of these new capital offenses threatened either the newly consolidated private property of the gentry class (petty theft, highway robbery, trespassing, and poaching), or the power of the state to ensure and underwrite the commodity value of coinage and paper money (clipping, coining, counterfeiting, and forging). Defined by economic historian Peter Linebaugh (2003) as a "thanatocracy" (50), the Bloody Code defined the basic power of English sovereignty in terms of both the broad exercise of the death penalty and its particular exercise in situations where the symbolic and state-sanctioned value of money required dramatic enforcement. For example, after the Coinage Act of 1696, the simple (and illegal) process of cutting back the edges of an English coin to extract from the weight of the original token joined the assembly of felonies punished by public hanging. Similarly, the hunting of fowl on a squire's land and the acquisition of extra coals from his weekly delivery—both traditional forms of in-kind payment for labor before the imposition of the Bloody Code—became hanging offenses under the emerging modern capitalist regime.

With capital punishment embraced as the primary form of sanction during the eighteenth century, imprisonment served a minority of offenses, accounting for only 2.3 percent of English judges' sentences during the 1770s (Ignatieff 1978: 15). Most of these carceral sentences required terms of a year or less and were imposed on a strictly narrow range of noncapital offenses including manslaughter, commercial fraud, perjury, union action, and public rioting.

In England, modern prison reform began with John Howard, a Bedfordshire County sheriff, who conducted tours of existing gaols and debtors' houses during the 1770s and 1780s (McGowen 1998: 78–80). His published report *The State of the Prisons of England and Wales* (1784 [1777]) detailed a hideous carnival of deprivation and debasement occurring behind prison walls. Howard meticulously documented vermin-infested subterranean dungeons awash with human filth, indiscriminate mingling of male and female inmates, and desperate paupers rotting in chains unable to afford the food bribes required by corrupt gaolers. The vast majority of these pre-reform gaols were adapted from preexisting medieval fortifications (Brodie et al. 2002). Recycled structures typically consisted of castle keeps—the Tower of London, Cambridge County Gaol and Bridewell, Launceston County Gaol, Chester County Gaol, Lancaster County

Figure 2.1. Ypres Castle, Rye, England, 2006. (Photograph by Eleanor Casella.)

Gaol, Windsor Debtors' Prison, and Lincoln Castle Prison—or gatehouses of city walls—York Gaol, Newcastle County Gaol, Bristol Newgate, Carmarthen Borough Gaol, Ypres Castle of Rye (figure 2.1), and London Newgate, the most infamous of all eighteenth-century prisons (Evans 1982: 12).

Designed to enforce containment itself as a form of punishment and deterrence, these early prisons were internally divided to accommodate only three types of residents—debtors, felons, and misdemeanants (Brodie et al. 2002). Consisting mostly of insolvent tradesmen and householders, debtors comprised approximately half of the English prison population. Since felons were typically sentenced to death, corporeal punishment, or transportation to penal settlements in North America (and later Australia), those incarcerated were typically held for relatively short periods while awaiting assize trial or execution of final sentence. Misdemeanants comprised a class of petty offenders sentenced for short periods of corrective discipline—primarily disobedient apprentices and servants, prostitutes, and vagabonds caught outside their home parishes. While specific accommodation differed dramatically between the eighteenth-century gaols and bridewells, general patterns indicate that felons experienced the harshest conditions, debtors paid the highest prices for their own maintenance, and misdemeanants experienced the greatest degree of protoinstitutional discipline (Evans 1982: 19–21).

The underlying hardship shared by all three prisoner castes was the cost of maintenance within the gaol. Appointed by the local magistrate or aldermen, "keepers" were essentially contractors licensed to prevent escapes. In exchange, they were permitted to charge prisoners for all aspects of accommodation—food, bedding, clothing, visitation allowances, removal of slops, and even removal of heavy irons, shackles, and chains. Prisons were essentially run as privatized and rather lucrative hostels, with monopolistic fees levied for every kind of provision and every form of privilege (McGowen 1998: 72–75). Strong liquor, tea, coffee, chocolate, lace, velvet, fresh fruit and vegetables, fish, poultry, and a colorful array of sexual gratifications could be obtained during incarceration—for the right price. Within the confines of the perimeter walls, the largest gaols included stalls and taverns subcontracted by the keeper:

> At Newgate in the early eighteenth century there were at least three distinct places for the purchase of consumables: the cellar, run by a prisoner, the "cellarman," supplying wine, brandy, beer, tobacco, candles and other requisites to better off felons; the taphouse, selling the same range of goods to poorer felons; and the lodge, providing for debtors. The taphouse and lodge were leased by the gaoler to external proprietors. (Evans 1982: 28)

While this monopolistic relationship between gaolers and prisoners was open to blatant abuse, the power of the keeper was in practice limited by the socioeconomic links they were required to maintain with prisoners, their primary (if involuntary) source of income. In contrast to the situation in later reformed prisons, gaolers' livelihoods depended on prisoners rather than on boards of magistrates or state authorities. The flow of goods, visitors, tradesmen, and information through the perimeter walls thus provided the major source of profit for gaolers, encouraging vigilant taxation and control of such trafficking rather than its strict prohibition. Prominently displayed lists of fees structured the penal experience far more than disciplinary rules or regulations. For those who could not afford services, the fundamental cruelties of extortion, destitution, illness, and starvation accompanied imprisonment. By the late eighteenth century, the English prison was popularly reputed to be an "Abominable sink of beastliness" (qtd. in Evans 1982: 34).

The outbreak of hostilities in the North American colonies in 1775 suspended all criminal transportation across the Atlantic, forcing authorities in the Home Office to develop alternative forms of punishment for convicted felons. The 1777 publication of John Howard's comprehensive survey of gaols had relentlessly exposed the worst horrors of England's penal system to Parliament. Growing concern over the morality of corporeal punishment became expressed in legal prohibitions of branding, whipping, and chaining confined felons. By 1800, even the number of death penalties to reach actual execution in London had dropped to a little over 10 percent (Ignatieff 1978: 90).

Social and moral pressures eventually combined to spur an interest in new forms of "reformed" penitentiary architecture—particularly Jeremy Bentham's designs, described in his 1791 *Panopticon; or the Inspection House*. An elite British industrialist, Bentham developed an obsession with an architecture of utopian surveillance modeled after the factory his brother Samuel had devised for Prince Potemkin and Catherine the Great of Russia during the late 1780s (Semple 1993: 99; Evans 1982: 196). As Michel Foucault dramatically theorized (1977), Bentham's institutional designs emphasized disciplinary rehabituation of the mind over retributive punishment of the flesh. While Bentham devised his "inspection house" to enforce the traditional goals of punishment, deterrence, and reformation, three new concepts entered his reformed institutional scheme: lenity, severity, and parsimony (Semple 1993: 112). Imprisonment was meant to deprive the inmate solely of liberty, not of health or life. Thus, while a severe discipline was to be both certain and routine, the prisoner would never be starved, overworked, or beaten. Regular provision of food rations and uniforms would confirm a minimum standard of humane care for the inmate. While accommodation would be kept economical to support the continued financial viability of the penitentiary, a basic level of sanitation, warmth, and sustenance would be provided to ensure inmates' health.

And yet, the Panopticon offered a rigorous new technology of punishment. Described by Foucault as a "cruel and ingenious cage" (1977: 205), Bentham's penitential designs delineated a pitiless contraption of cast iron and glass fabricated solely for the physical and psychological subjugation of its inhabitants. The Panopticon's fundamental architecture became a mechanism for generating morality. Designed as a ring of open cells arranged in a circumference around a central inspection tower, the penitentiary was intended to provide guards with complete surveillance over all activities and communications in the institution (figure 2.2). Large glazed windows would light the cells by day, and reflector-mounted lamps would be used to cast light into each cell during the night.

Bentham's original design also included "conversation tubes" installed between the central tower and each cell (Semple 1993: 117). Functioning as a disciplinary communications system, the tubes would enable the prison governor to instruct and admonish each inmate while maintaining his complete anonymity and isolation. Thus, the internal architectural relationships themselves created a unique state of institutional confinement:

Bentham laid down the principle that power should be visible and un-verifiable. Visible: the inmate will constantly have before his eyes the tall outline of the central tower from which he is spied upon. Unverifi-able: the inmate must never know whether he is being looked at any one moment; but he must be sure that he may always be so. (Foucault 1977: 201)

Hence, the major purpose of Bentham's Panopticon was to transfer the exercise of subordination to the inmates themselves. The penitentiary was a laboratory, a machine for experimentally altering behavior, for training and correcting individuals. Over the course of incarceration, reform was achieved by forcing prisoners to internalize the prison's disciplinary regime as they adjusted under the constant threat of discovery. Foucault inventories these coercive power dynamics:

So to arrange things that the surveillance is permanent in its effects, even if it is discontinuous in its action; that the perfection of power should tend to render its actual exercise unnecessary; that this architectural apparatus should be a machine for creating and sustaining a power relation independent of the person who exercises it; in short, that the inmates should be caught up in a power situation of which they are themselves the bearers. (1977: 201)

In direct contrast to practice in actual eighteenth-century prisons, Panopticon inmates were to be kept in constant solitude so as to thwart both the emergence of dangerous associations and the expression of rebellious solidarity. Rather than relying on extortion, fees, and bribes, the underlying economic foundation of the Panopticon was to be industry. Inmates were to labor sixteen hours a day alone in their cells. Channeled back to the prison contractor, profits based on solitary industry ensured that his livelihood remained independent of any social relationship with the incarcerated. By 1791, Bentham's concept of the Panopticon had emerged as a sublime model for institutional confinement, as a terrible machine for "grinding rogues honest" (Evans 1982: 198). Over the next thirty years, Bentham obsessively revised his designs while tirelessly lobbying the British parliament to fund the construction of his utopian scheme.

Rise of the Prison in the New Republic

As previously noted, no specific institutions existed in colonial America to impose punishment on eighteenth-century lawbreakers. Based on English common law, colonial-era criminal codes relied heavily on traditional punitive practices—on mechanisms of shame (the stocks, pillory, or public cage);

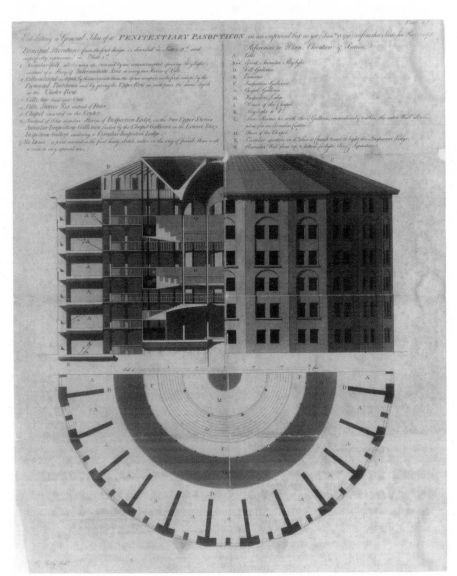

Figure 2.2. The "Penitentiary Panopticon." (Drawing by architect Willey Reveley after Samuel Bentham's design; commissioned by Jeremy Bentham for *Panopticon, or House of Inspection*, 1791. Reproduced by permission of University College London, Library Services, Bentham Papers.)

on afflictive penalties (whipping, flogging, and branding); on fining, banishment, or hanging—to modify or deter deviant behaviors. In common with eighteenth-century Britain, a sentence of imprisonment was rarely used as a form of punishment in itself. Local jails and lockups tended to contain those awaiting judgment or execution of sentence rather than those undergoing correctional sentences. However, by the end of the Revolutionary War in 1783, a combination of demographic and economic influences combined to undermine the efficacy of these traditional modes of punishment and social control.

In his classic historical study of American asylums (1990), David Rothman links the development of new criminal theories of rehabilitation to post-Revolutionary republican ideologies of citizenship, liberty, and meritocratic opportunity. In the aftermath of independence and nationhood, American legislators and social leaders linked the persistence of social deviance to the archaic, brutal, arbitrary, and unenlightened British codes that had informed colonial-era criminal law. To strengthen social order, the new American government redesigned legislation to make punishments moderate, rehabilitative, regularly applied, and strictly enforced. Thus, the first stage of American criminological reform was primarily legislative, not penitential. Incarceration as a punishment in itself provided a more optimistic and humane option than hanging and a less brutal form than whipping. The intended outcome was reclamation of the productive citizen. A period of confinement was expected to deter future acts of deviancy or dependence—particularly in the case of female offenders, a group less likely to earn the hangman's sentence.

As statutes restricted the death penalty to a limited number of serious or violent offenses, state legislatures began to approve funds for construction of new jails throughout the republic. Pennsylvania led the movement, completing the repair and expansion of the Walnut Street Prison by 1795 (figure 2.3) (Cotter et al. 1988). The renovation of the Walnut Street Prison from a local jail to a state institution therefore represented not only the first American attempt at establishing a penitentiary (Friedman 1993), but also the first manifestation of a centralized state-run apparatus in the New Republic (Garman 1999; Takagi 1993). Over the following five years, state prisons were established in New York (1796), New Jersey (1797), and Virginia and Kentucky (both 1800). By the start of the nineteenth century, funds for prison construction had been approved by legislatures in Massachusetts, Vermont, New Hampshire, and Maryland (Rothman 1990: 61).

Other scholars also trace late eighteenth-century American criminological reform to demographic and philosophical sources, arguing that the emergence of penitentiaries in the New Republic was an evolutionary, rather than a revolutionary, phenomenon (Henretta 1973: 169). As Adam Hirsch points

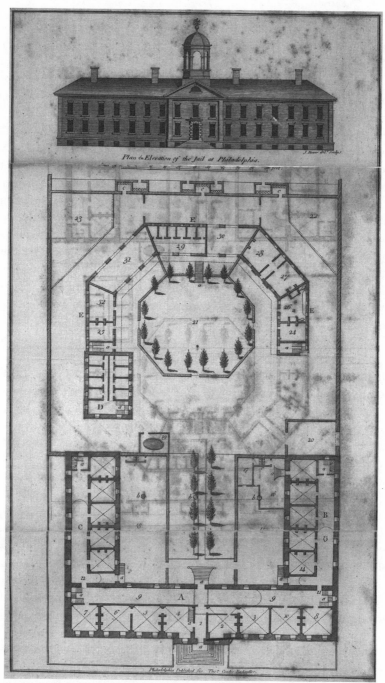

Figure 2.3. Plan and elevation of the jail at Philadelphia. Upper plan, prison workshops (excavated 1973); lower plan, cell block. (Drawn and engraved by Joseph Bowes. *Philadelphia Monthly Magazine*, volume 1, February 1798. Reproduced by permission of the Library Company of Philadelphia.)

out (1992), the social and economic impact of the American Revolution contributed to changes in the disposition of criminal punishment. The war years 1776–83 brought a new degree of mobility to American populations. As a result of diminished community insularity, traditional public punishments no longer held the same potency as means of retribution or deterrence. At the same time, the successful revolution deprived Americans of their traditional British imperial markets, and a lengthy period of economic depression followed the general commercial dislocation of the 1780s (Nettels 1962). Following 1783, the demobilization of troops increased unemployment and crime throughout the New Republic. In addition to these war-related disruptions, changing social patterns and general dissatisfaction with traditional criminal sanctions had already emerged earlier in the eighteenth century. Indeed, Massachusetts, Pennsylvania, and Connecticut were developing incarceration programs during the decade *before* independence (Hirsch 1992: 55–56), although their penal reforms were abruptly halted by the outbreak of hostilities with Britain. Thus, the emergence of the state prison during the first decades of the New Republic may represent a return to pre-Revolutionary reforms rather than a radical new departure.

But regardless of its specific origins, various forms of institutional confinement proliferated over the period. The early years of the American republic witnessed the establishment of prisons and jails throughout the eastern states. However, unlike penitentiaries of the nineteenth century, these early American institutions utilized confinement itself as a compassionate form of punishment—as a humane and rational alternative to the gallows. The radical idea that the internal organization of institutional space could *itself* be harnessed for reformatory purposes would await a subsequent generation.

The Golden Age of the American Institution

With the Jacksonian era of the 1830s, institutional forms of social welfare became emblazoned on the national landscape. As a "carceral enthusiasm" (Hirsch 1992: 66) swept the country, confinement emerged as the primary mode of accommodation for the poor, the disabled, and the criminal. Over the course of this decade, a profound and optimistic belief in the power of architecture as a moral science gripped the young nation. Intended as mechanisms for the cultivation of virtue, these vigorous new institutions harnessed the built environment not only to contain those judged dangerous or desperate, but to rectify their civic characters—to transform their mortal souls.

Americans further embraced new progressive social policies designed to scientifically structure the rehabilitation of aberrant behaviors. Increasing urban migration, particularly throughout the northern states, drove what Garman and Russo (1999) call a "mayhem of industrialization" (120) as a new class of landless migrants moved between towns seeking factory employment. Their growing numbers enflamed public fears about the corrupting influence of the "lower orders." Philanthropic reformers urged their respective state legislatures to combat the "multiplying temptations to crime" (Dix 1845: 25) that had led to increasing rates of vagrancy, poverty, deviance, and mental illness. Since such aberration, argued Jacksonian reformers, resulted from contaminating association with deviants, reform could be achieved only by their removal from the general social milieu. Thus, the desire to separate out and thereby improve such unproductive citizens quickly collapsed earlier eighteenth-century criticisms of the function, cost, and practicality of institutional confinement: "Just as the penitentiary would reform the criminal and the insane asylum would cure the mentally ill, so the almshouse would rehabilitate the poor" (Rothman 1990: 180).

By the end of Jackson's second administration in 1837, establishments for the deviant and the dependent multiplied across the nation as confinement became the central mode of both publicly and privately funded social management. In Massachusetts, sixty new municipal almshouses were constructed between 1820 and 1840 (Rothman 1990: 183), and in Rhode Island fifteen new rural institutions for the poor had been erected across the state by 1850 (Hazard 1973 [1851]: 64–65). New York witnessed a similar proliferation. By 1835, all but four of the state's fifty-five counties had established a poorhouse (Schneider 1938: 242). Between 1830 and 1860, Pennsylvania, Michigan, Ohio, and Illinois attempted to abolish outdoor relief programs by requiring the distribution of all aid support through municipal almshouses (Rothman 1990: 185). Although the laws proved controversial and unsustainable, they ensured that institutionalization dominated relief policies in these states.

Such carceral enthusiasm generated new architectural models designed to incorporate principles of surveillance, classification, separation, and discipline. Preexisting institutions underwent renovation programs to adapt or expand their structures according to nineteenth-century technologies of reform. Some architectural modifications were undertaken to enhance the spatial isolation of inmates from the outside world, as in the case of a new rear building added for "the most unrepentant" women to the Magdalen Asylum of Philadelphia in 1832 (De Cunzo 1995: 46). Other adaptations were undertaken to provide separate accommodation for different types of inmates. In 1824, for example, the Falmouth Almshouse of Massachusetts added internal walls to partition communal dormitories into individual cells (Strauss and Spencer-Wood 1999). Similarly, an additional structure for housing mentally ill paupers was erected

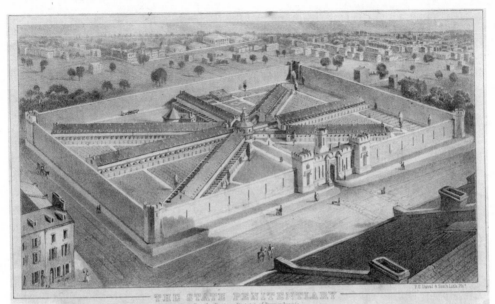

Figure 2.4. The state penitentiary for the eastern district of Pennsylvania (detail). (James Fuller Queen artist; P. S. Duval and Son publisher, ca. 1858. Reproduced by permission of the Library Company of Philadelphia.)

at Rhode Island's Smithfield Town Farm and Asylum in 1854 (Garman and Russo 1999: 122–23).

The primary architectural innovation during this golden era of the institution was the radial plan, a design adapted from Jeremy Bentham's eighteenth-century Panopticon. The classic penitential radial plan provided accommodation for inmates in cells, typically grouped into blocks along tall open corridors. These narrow wings were arranged as spokes around a central observatory structure that held the guardhouse and often the chapel. Between the wings, walled exercise yards radiated from the core structure to the perimeter wall, yielding a circular or octagonal plan that closely resembled a wheel (figure 2.4). The first American radial penitentiary was established for male offenders at Cherry Hill, Philadelphia (1829). Also known as the Eastern State Penitentiary, the facility was designed with individual cells for convicts, each connected to one of the small exercise yards to maximize inmate isolation (Friedman 1993: 79). Various types of institutions of this period incorporated elements of the new disciplinary architecture. By the 1850s, asylums for the insane, for example, typically consisted of a central administrative structure of several stories, frequently decorated by an observation balcony or "cupola of height and distinction," with plain and repetitious wings of rooms for male and female patients radiating from its sides (Rothman 1990: 153).

However, it was the new reformed penitentiaries for men in Pennsylvania and New York that most explicitly embraced the radial plan as key to the new corrective enterprise. To "soften the mind" to virtuous suggestion (Ignatieff 1978: 74), the male penitentiary inmate was architecturally subjected to forms of sensory deprivation combined with unpredictable yet frequent direct surveillance. Not only were his bodily movements choreographed by daily musters, inspection parades, and labor routines, but the inmate's basic embodied experience was determined by the material world of the penitentiary. Inmate isolation, a central feature in the original Benthamite model, was enforced through a strict regimen of silence. The radial plan channeled sounds from cell blocks toward the central guards' quarters. Stray noises and communication attempts were amplified by the long empty corridors and vaulted ceilings, thereby enhancing auditory surveillance over inmates (Upton 1992: 66–69). Spy holes were built into each cell door. Covered by a flap on the corridor side, they exposed the cell interior to inspection, while limiting inmate views of the external hall. Walls and grated windows circumscribed all views of the outside world.

Textiles and furnishings were similarly restricted. To humiliate and discipline male inmates, identity numbers and coarse wool and cotton uniforms obscured expressions of individual identity. First adopted in state prisons of the New Republic to increase institutional hygiene and decrease chances of escape from public labor assignments, the prison uniform by the nineteenth century had itself become part of the disciplinary ritual through which the convict became institutionalized. Cells were sparsely furnished with identical artifact sets: tin cup, bowl, and spoon; cot, blanket, chamber pot, and broom; a bible and a framed list of institutional rules and regulations.

From the 1820s, two rival American philosophies of incarceration—the congregate and the separate—competed to determine the character of the penitentiary as a distinctive sociocultural environment. Over the next thirty years, vitriolic debates and passionate campaigns broadcast in periodicals, public speeches, and philanthropic pamphlets drew international attention and tourists to the new "palaces for felons" (Ignatieff 1978: 3). Given European curiosity over innovative American carceral designs, foreign visitors included official state investigators appointed by France, England, and Prussia (Beaumont and Tocqueville 1965 [1833]). Although with historical hindsight the similarities between the two schemes far outweighed the differences, the debates themselves gained significance by revealing the underlying technologies of, and popular enthusiasm for, institutional confinement during the Jacksonian era (Hirsch 1992: 92).

For both systems, institutionalization's promise of prisoner reform depended on strict isolation and disciplinary routine. In contrast with earlier eighteenth-century attempts to reclaim unproductive citizens by deterring them from undesirable acts, institutional confinement in the 1830s became a *rehabituative* practice, one intended to create a progressive and internalized transformation of the male criminal. Silence would isolate inmates from each other; constant and routine activities would rehabituate the convict to less offensive lifeways. The internal, material world of the institution would therefore be harnessed as a primary tool of rehabilitation. With the penitentiary embraced as a technology for the improvement of civil society, reformers turned their new institutional experiments in the "moral sciences" toward the outside world. Debates between supporters of the two systems raged passionately:

> Nothing less than the safety and future stability of the republic was at issue, the triumph of good over evil, of order over chaos. Intense partisanship was natural where the right program would reform the criminal and reorder the society, and the wrong one would encourage vice and crime. (Rothman 1990: 85)

New York initiated the debate by establishing the Auburn or "congregate system" for its state penitentiaries at Auburn (1823) and Ossining (1825), or "Sing-Sing" as it became infamously nicknamed. In this first American system, male prisoners were separately incarcerated within their cells by night and silently labored together in prison workshops by day (Lewis 1965). A rival carceral approach known as the "separate system" was devised in Pennsylvania for the Western State Penitentiary of Pittsburgh (1826) and the Eastern State Penitentiary of Philadelphia at Cherry Hill (1829). Drawn more closely from Jeremy Bentham's institutional philosophies, the Pennsylvania system enforced the complete isolation of the male prisoner for his term of incarceration (Teeters and Shearer 1957). Inmates slept, ate, and worked within the confines of their individual cells, emerging only to undertake solitary exercise within one of the enclosed courtyards. Wardens and prisoners were assigned boots with soft leather soles to prevent the sound of footsteps from echoing along the long corridors of the radial plan. At the Eastern State Penitentiary, a hood was placed over the head of the male inmate whenever he left his cell to maintain his anonymity and to limit possibilities for nonverbal communication with other inmates.

To choreograph the complete isolation of inmates, the minute division and regulation of time and space were required. Thus, rancorous arguments between each system's supporters focused on elements of architecture and material culture utilized by each one. Advocates of the Pennsylvania system decried the incomplete isolation of inmates under the Auburn system of congregated labor, believing it to result in diminished rehabilitation. Auburn supporters claimed that Pennsylvania's penitentiaries were incapable of enforcing their program of total isolation and suggested faults in the design of solitary cells. In response, cell wall thickness and water levels in each cell's toilet were carefully calculated and published for the Eastern State Penitentiary to demonstrate that inmates could not use a Morse Code of taps for illicit communication (Upton 1992: 66). Auburn supporters countered with accusations that the architecture itself bred insanity.

Underlying the rhetoric and passion lay a primary question about the nature of labor in places of institutional confinement. While the Pennsylvania system adopted an idealistic Benthamite approach emphasizing the rehabilitative qualities of isolation over economic productivity, the Auburn approach developed a daily routine focused on productive labor to simultaneously advance both economic and reformist goals. Despite initial qualms over its similarities with forms of African-American slavery then practiced in the southern states, the financial pragmatism of New York's Auburn system quickly won the sympathies of other states across both North and South (Hirsch 1992; Tomlinson 1980). By 1835, Auburn-type penitentiaries had been constructed in Connecticut, Massachusetts, Maryland, Vermont, Louisiana, and Virginia (Garland 1990; Rothman 1990). With expansion of the American state after mid-century, newly established prisons of the American West continued this national diffusion of the Auburn system (Friedman 1993; Hauff 1988). Although the profits generated by prison industries never balanced against the construction and operational costs of America's Auburn-type penitentiaries, the concept of labor as a mandatory, disciplinary, and income-generating activity served as a central component of institutional confinement over the following century.

Keeping the Fallen: On the Nature of Women's Confinement

Although some elements of the Jacksonian-era penitential regime were applied to female inmates—the assignment of uniforms and identification numbers; the regulation of food, resources, and access throughout the compound; and the enforcement of hard and repetitive labor duties—the strict isolation of the Auburn and Pennsylvania systems was rarely applied in women's wards of the new penal institutions. Constituting less than 4 percent of the total inmate population in 1850 (Friedman 1993: 233), female convicts tended to be accommodated either in shared cells or in dormitory-style wards established in penal institutions intended for men (Upton 1992). For example, during the 1850s the Louisiana State Penitentiary at Baton Rouge set aside "two large unfinished rooms, occupied in common by women and children" (Wurtzburg and Hahn 1992a: 5). Over the nineteenth century, solitary confinement served more as a temporary method of secondary punishment for female offenders rather than as a primary mode of incarceration.

No independent prisons were built solely for incarceration of women before 1870 (Friedman 1993). During the nineteenth and early twentieth centuries, female criminals tended to be arrested for opportunistic property crimes (petty larceny) or, less frequently, for specifically gender-linked criminal activities (public drunkenness, prostitution, adultery, and infanticide or abortion). As a result, women tended to be incarcerated in county jails and houses of correction rather than in state penitentiaries.

Some "administratively dependent" prisons for women were constructed within the boundaries of larger male institutional compounds, such as the Mount Pleasant Female Prison established in 1839 as a satellite of the Ossining State Penitentiary (Sing-Sing) in New York (Friedman 1993: 233; Freedman 1981: 48). Overseen by male administrators, its internal functions were served by female matrons who maintained sanitary conditions and provided some measure of disciplinary order. Although the prison was plagued by overcrowding, deficient hospital and nursery facilities, and persistent disciplinary problems, Mount Pleasant remained the only American dedicated female prison until the 1870s.

In contrast to male inmates, women's hard labor generally occurred inside the boundaries of the perimeter wall, and an expiration of sentence was typically followed by assignment to a halfway house or "refuge" for a further period of regimented labor rather than by conditional release to the outside world (Freedman 1981). In other words, female inmates tended to experience a greater array of institutional forms than their male counterparts. Even into the early decades of the twentieth century, places of confinement established for women commonly operated as multifunctional institutions, providing hospital care, poor relief, refuge assistance, basic literacy skills, vocational training, parenting education, and employment services in addition to basic penal confinement (Rafter 1990). Further, the conditional release schemes designed for most female inmates resulted in their transfer from a state-run prison to an equally institutional reformatory or asylum run by a religious or voluntary society, thereby blurring the experiential boundaries between types of institutional confinement (De Cunzo 2001).

To further intensify the ambiguous complexity of these carceral institutions, women's prisons also managed the confinement of an additional population of nonoffenders—the dependent infants and children of inmates. If a woman was nursing or pregnant at the time of commitment (or became pregnant while incarcerated), her child was typically allowed institutional residency for an initial two to five years. With the establishment of dedicated female prisons over the late nineteenth century, accommodation of these dependent residents frequently resulted in the creation of segregated nursery wards within institutions—arguably required to promote a safe and hygienic environment for the infants. However, access to these special wards was usually restricted, either through the logistics of daily work regimes or through policies that defined such contact as a privilege and linked it to the mother's compliance with institutional regulations. This practice of familial disruption, when combined with the inevitable removal of the weaned child from the institution, served as a powerful device for the social control of female inmates (Rafter 1990; Dobash et al. 1986; Freedman 1981; for comparative analysis, see Damousi 1997, and Zedner 1991). Struggling under their Victorian (and patriarchal) assumptions about humane accommodation, modes of labor, and provision of infant care, nineteenth- and early twentieth-century penal administrators and philanthropic reformers alike found female convicts a source of perpetual confusion and frustration (Dobash et al. 1986).

A Cruel and Ingenious Cage: Critiques at Mid-century

By 1850, institutions had been founded throughout the country to care for the mentally ill, to rehabilitate criminals, to treat the disabled, and to educate the young. Most American states and territories maintained an Auburn-style prison, and most municipalities supported at least one multicomponent institution for poor relief. Accommodating some combination of male and female inmates, this latter establishment was variously described as an "almshouse" or "house of refuge" in documentary accounts referring to the deserving poor it housed and as a "workhouse," "house of industry," or "town farm" when residents were classified as undeserving or vagrant. Thus, by mid-century the poorhouse had transformed from a place of respite into an institution of social policy. Co-opting popular reformist philosophies from the flourishing state penitentiary systems, American asylums for poor relief were designed to remove individuals from "the corrupting, tempting and distracting influences of the world long enough for a kind but firm regimen to transform their behavior and reorder their personalities" (Katz 1986: 11).

Certainty of the general rehabilitative power of labor emerged as the central distinguishing characteristic of mid-century institutional confinement. The most infamous example of this blind faith consisted of meaningless and punitive forms of labor such as the treadmill, rock breaking, or oakum picking—a particularly odious task involving the tearing apart of salt and tar encrusted hemp ropes donated from local maritime industries. Nonetheless, although such regimented activities could be enforced upon an inmate population, they were rarely economically productive. Biased toward repetitive and unskilled activities, institutionalized labor proved uncompetitive in the production of commodities (Garman 2005). The lengthy periods required to obtain, install, or upgrade necessary facilities and machinery for production prevented workhouses and prisons from responding to changes in manufacturing technology or prevailing fashion. Few of the governing authorities, whether boards of directors or state wardens, were financially savvy businessmen. Thus, despite the initial enthusiasm for inmate labor as a simultaneous source of rehabilitation and profit, institutional confinement never became an economically profitable system.

By the second half of the century, the spiraling cost of institutionalization began to foment critique throughout America. An ever-increasing inmate population, coupled with a lack of evidence for the revolutionary moral transformations promised by Jacksonian-era reformers, began to erode the social optimism of the previous generation. From the 1850s, a more ambivalent vision of institutional confinement began to emerge. Asylums and prisons throughout American became regarded as overcrowded, corrupt, and brutal warehouses for the depraved, diseased, and desperate on the fringes of society. But despite this creeping disillusionment, institutional confinement had become fully established as the primary mode of social management for disenfranchised populations of men and women. Over the next five decades, institutionalization was applied to an increasingly diverse range of vulnerable groups in American society.

A Crisis of Citizenship: Confinement and the Neutralization of Dissent

The outbreak of hostilities during the Civil War brought a new mode of institutional confinement to America. Although treason laws had generated a small population of political prisoners prior to this national rift, the vast majority of men and women confined from the colonial through the Jacksonian periods had been convicted of either nonproductive or law-breaking behaviors. While such dependent or deviant activities demanded correction, the inmate's underlying relationship to the American nation-state did not come under scrutiny. Indeed, as earlier noted, Rothman (1990) links the adoption of institutional confinement, as a humane alternative to capital punishment, to the revolutionary philosophies of citizenship and nationhood forged in the early republic. When confined within an institution, the inmate was by definition the responsibility of the American state. As foreign-born immigrants, particularly Irish and German arrivals, came to dominate the population of county almshouses and workhouses by the 1850s, Americans of the propertied classes began to view custodial care as the most appropriate (albeit grim and grossly inadequate) method of accommodating the needy (Rothman 1990: 292–94). Even so, intrinsic issues of responsibility and "national identity" went unchallenged: the state maintained a basic duty of care for these new Americans.

With the outbreak of civil war, the traditional concept of "the citizen" disintegrated as Americans expressed allegiance to one of two directly competing models of national governance. The establishment of prisons for captured enemy soldiers resulted in the first application of institutional confinement to new categories of ambiguously defined noncitizens who were neither criminal nor destitute. Over the subsequent 140 years, institutional confinement was embraced as a primary management strategy for American communities and subcultures defined as ethnically, racially, or politically anomalous to mainstream society.

Civil War–period institutional confinement differed from previous types in another significant respect. Jeremy Bentham's original eighteenth-century Panopticon designs had adopted elements of military practice as a central component of institutionalization (Rothman 1990: 105; Foucault 1977: 151–56), but while Civil War prisons for captured enemy soldiers explicitly utilized this quasi-military model, they also introduced a new objective. Previous types of carceral institutions used military regimentation to inculcate strict discipline, precision, labor efficiency, and docile obedience in inmates—all to accomplish their ultimate rehabituation as productive citizens. In contrast, American Civil War prisons abandoned the reformist aim of antebellum asylums, poorhouses, and penitentiaries, offering instead a method of population warehousing that precluded social rehabilitation or moral improvement.

By 1861, both the Confederate and Federal governments had accepted the likelihood of a lengthy war and consequently made plans for long-term accommodation of the thousands of enemy prisoners under their jurisdiction. While some encampments, such as the Union prison at Johnson's Island, Ohio (1862–65), were established to isolate officers from enlisted men (Bush 2000), others, including the infamous Confederate prison at Andersonville, Georgia (1864–65), and its equally brutal Union cognate in Elmira, New York (1864–65), provided general confinement for captured soldiers undifferentiated by rank (Prentice and Prentice 2000). Surrounded by a stockade of wooden posts and earthworks, the compounds were originally intended to consist of either single- or two-story barracks of uniform dimensions and appearance arranged in linear fashion around a central yard or parade ground (Prentice and Prentice 2000: 168; Bush 2000: 64). However, extreme overcrowding and deprivation, as documented in period photographs and survivor accounts, tended to overwhelm any effective use of such military-style architecture. Indeed, as chapter 4 will detail, at the Confederate prison of Camp Ford, East Texas (1863–65), prisoners were expected to construct their own accommodation of "log shanties" and "wigwams," although African-American slaves from local properties were assigned to build the surrounding log post stockade (Thoms 2004: 77–78).

Thus, institutional accommodation in this explicitly military context was undertaken not to transform inmates into better soldiers, but to warehouse captured enemy combatants at the least expense until they could be exchanged. During the course of the Civil War, approximately 420,000 soldiers were incarcerated as prisoners of war (Hesseltine 1930: 2). By 1865, the American experience of institutional confinement had expanded to include a form of exile *within* the national territory. A new mode of institutionalization designed for the storage of ambiguously defined noncitizens had been introduced. This dramatic shift in the explicit aims, objectives, and subjects of institutional confinement marked an end to the golden era of the institution in America.

Under Continuous Discipline: The Convict Leasing System and Indian Boarding School Movement

Following the end of the Civil War, issues of ethnicity and race infused new tensions over "citizenship" as the cessation of African-American slavery and westward expansion into Native American territories increasingly diversified the population of the rapidly growing nation. Over subsequent decades, leaders in government, business, and social policy struggled to find a method for coping with demographic heterogeneity. How would these racially marginalized groups be integrated as patriotic and productive citizens? How could their labor be harnessed to support the demands of the booming industrial economy?

For African-Americans, these questions were overwhelmingly addressed through penal forms of confinement and labor assignment. Before the Civil War, most prisoners in the South were white; African-Americans were predominantly enslaved and punished by whipping or hanging rather than by incarceration. After 1865, Southern prisons filled with African-Americans, specifically young black men (Carleton 1971; McKelvey 1936). In 1871, the 828 prisoners incarcerated in Virginia's state penitentiary consisted of 609 black men, 63 black women, 152 white men, and 4 white women. As of early October 1899, the entire population of state prisoners in Georgia totaled 2,201, of which 1,885 were black men and 68 were black women. Only 245 white men and 3 white women were included in this inmate population (Friedman 1993: 156).

Economically and politically devastated by postwar reconstruction, the Southern states resorted to a convict leasing system and plantation prisons to relieve the fiscal burden of managing both the crumbling antebellum-era prisons and expanding inmate population. Thus, in most parts of the South, Auburn-style industrial prisons were abandoned in favor of private leasing contracts. Prisoners were housed in work camps and served as unfree labor in mines, swamps, cotton fields, and on railroads (Novak 1978; Carleton 1971). As large numbers of former slaves entered the prison system with long sentences, institutional confinement became in practice a legal manifestation of slavery (Christianson 1998; B. Foster 1995; McKelvey 1936). As large mining and railroad companies competed with smaller regional businesses to win convict leases, inmate death rates soared. Between 1877 and 1880, of the 285 mostly African-American convicts assigned in Georgia to build the Greenwood and Augusta Railroad, approximately 45 percent died (Friedman 1993: 95). While death rates in the Virginia state penitentiary averaged 1.5 percent during the 1880s, they rose to over 11 percent at work camps operated by contractors for the Richmond and Allegheny Railroad (Friedman 1993: 157).

In stark contrast to the criminalization and privatized incarceration of African-Americans, social reformers of the late nineteenth century paradoxically returned to embrace the transformative effects of institutional confinement when scrutinizing the indigenous tribal communities of the American West. In other words, as policy makers grew skeptical of the rehabilitative value of confinement in relation to the nation's existing prisons and asylums, they simultaneously exhibited a blind faith in its value as an instrument for transforming Native Americans into westernized citizens. Prevailing reformist ideology dictated that social transformation could be cultivated through the institutional application of proper education, training, and discipline—an optimistic philosophy that informed debates over the architectural design of American schoolhouses from mid-century (Gibb and Beisaw 2000; Markus 1993; Preston 1992; Peña 1992). By removing Indian children from their families on the reservations and immersing them in the values and practical knowledge of American society, philanthropists believed they could be culturally assimilated—transformed into patriotic and productive citizens. They would emerge as self-sufficient workers no longer dependent on the meager levels of federal support grudgingly administered through the Bureau of Indian Affairs (Trennert 1988). Certainty about the rehabilitative power of labor, both as a

Table 2.1. Sample Daily Routine, Cushman Indian School, Tacoma, Washington, Monday, February 1, 1912

5:45 a.m.	Reveille
5:55–6:10	Setting up exercises and drill
6:12	Air beds
6:12–6:45	Recreation
6:45	First call for breakfast
6:55	Assembly and roll call
7:00	Breakfast
7:30–7:35	Care of teeth
7:35–7:40	Make beds
7:40–7:55	Police quarters
7:55	Industrial call
8:00	Industrial work begins. School detail at liberty. The use of this period is at pupils' discretion. The more studious at books; those inclined to athletics make use of this time for practice. Some pupils practice music lessons, etc.
8:50	First school call; roll call and inspection
9:00	School
11:30	Recall; pupils at liberty
11:55	Assembly and roll call
12:00 p.m.	Dinner
12:30	Recreation
12:50	School and industrial call; inspection
1:00	Industrial work and school
3:30	School dismissed. School detail at liberty. Time spent in same general manner as morning detail utilizes period from 8:00 to 8:50.
4:30	Industrial recall; drill and gymnasium classes
5:15	First call
5:25	Assembly and roll call
5:30	Supper
6:00	Care of teeth
6:10	Recreation
7:15	First call
7:25	Roll call; inspection
7:30	Lecture. This period varies in length. Men prominent in education or civic affairs address the pupils.
8:15	Call to quarters. Older pupils prepare lessons; intermediate children play.
8:45	Tattoo; pupils retire
8:55	Check
9:00	Taps

means of implementing personal discipline and as a route to economic self-sufficiency, once again guided this new application of institutional confinement. Through domestic and vocational work, Indian children were expected to learn the value of personal possessions and individual wages. Coerced labor would furnish them with both the skills and desire to join the mainstream of American capitalist society.

Although many of the treaties negotiated with Native American tribes during the 1850s included some promise of educational support, no provision was made until after the Civil War. In 1879, the first off-reservation Indian boarding school was opened by Captain Richard Henry Pratt, an officer of the Tenth Cavalry who had commanded a unit of African-American soldiers and Indian scouts along the Texas and Oklahoma border. Drawing children from the Dakota, Kiowa, and Cheyenne nations, Pratt established his institution in an abandoned military post on the edge of Carlisle, Pennsylvania (Landis 1996). Explicitly adopting military practices such as dress uniforms, barrack-style accommodation, and daily marching drills, the Carlisle Indian Industrial School strove to "Kill the Indian, but save the Man" (Landis 1996). Staged "before-and-after" photographs of the Indian students were circulated through school newspapers and fundraising exhibits to visually demonstrate the profound influence of institutional confinement as an instrument for fostering cultural assimilation.

As Pratt's model became popular with government officials and wealthy East Coast benefactors, more than 100 off-reservation Indian boarding schools were founded across America, with the Chemawa Indian School (Salem, Oregon) and the Phoenix Indian School (Phoenix, Arizona) established as particularly large and regionally based multitribal institutions (Collins 1998; Trennert 1988). In 1893, Congress enacted a law establishing mandatory education for Indian children. Agents of the Bureau of Indian Affairs (BIA) were ordered to enforce this federal regulation on all children between the ages of eight and eighteen. Faced with a rapid expansion in the population of students confined within the government-run off-reservation schools, the BIA issued a series of directives to standardize institutional practices. By the turn of century, these included the adoption of military-style daily routines and dress uniforms, English-only language policies, mandatory labor assignments at agricultural work or domestic service, corporal punishment, and simultaneous training in academic and vocational skills (Adams 1995; Lomawaima 1994).

A typical daily schedule consisted of a series of strictly regulated tasks (table 2.1). Describing her time at the Tulalip Indian School in eastern Washington, Joyce Simmons Cheeka recalled:

Everything happened by bells, "triangles" they were called. A triangle would ring in the morning and we would all run, line up, march in, get our little quota of tooth powder, wash our teeth, brush our hair, wash our hands and faces, and then we all lined up and marched outside. Whether it was raining, snowing or blowing, we all went outside and did what was called "setting up exercises" for twenty minutes. (qtd. in Marr n.d.: 3)

Although days were supposed to be equally divided between academic instruction and vocation training, the latter was emphasized as educators believed a greater degree of economic independence would result from training in manual job skills. Vocational instruction was gendered according to Anglo-American norms (Lomawaima 1994). Girls were taught domestic skills, such as laundry, sewing, and cooking. Older girls were also allowed to train as nurses or office workers. Boys were educated in the various workshops that operated out of every boarding school, learning vocational skills such as wagon making, shoemaking, blacksmithing, tin working, carpentry, cabinet making, baking, and farm work. To reduce operating costs, schools were encouraged to implement an "outing system," whereby students were assigned to local farms or households as unpaid labor. This practice further reduced the quantity of academic education available to Indian students in the institutions.

Students did not always adapt to the harsh institutional environment of the industrial schools. Methods of coping ranged from open resistance to internalized accommodation. Archaeological evidence suggests that students tacitly retained a sense of Native American ethnicity by keeping and hiding fetishes, religious charms, and clan totems—objects that connected them to the customs and traditions of their homes (Lindauer 1996). Absconding from a boarding school resulted in public humiliation and periods of solitary confinement (Adams 1995: 222–38). A teacher at the Phoenix Indian School recollected:

Boys who were habitual weekend drunks, frequenters of Jefferson Street, or runaways were put in jail. There was an adobe building back of the present Navajo building, with a few small barred windows high in the walls. Some boys spent a lot of the school year there. When a runaway had repeated the offense several times, his head was shaved and he had to wear a dress to school on his dismissal from jail. A few boys hardly knew what pants were. (qtd. in Lindauer 1997: 45)

At the Chemawa Indian School, a former resident recounted the use of corporal punishment in response to an escape attempt:

Two of our girls ran away . . . but they got caught. They tied their legs up, tied their hands behind their backs, put them in the middle of the hallway so that if they fell, fell asleep or something, the matron would hear them and she'd get out there and whip them and make them stand up again. (qtd. in Marr n.d.: 4)

Critics of the off-reservation Indian boarding schools included some of the institutional educators. Estelle Aubrey Brown, employed by the Phoenix Indian School between 1915 and 1918, complained that the goal of providing the Indian child with tools for self-sufficiency remained unfulfilled:

> The deliberate aim of his education had been to unfit him for the only environment open to him—the reservation. There little of what he had been taught could be of use to him. At the school, boys were taught various trades, most of which were already outmoded. Of these trades, he was taught only a smattering. He could not compete successfully with white skilled labor. (1952: 218)

Despite marginal educational utility, institutional confinement as an instrument of cultural assimilation had a profound impact on Native American pupils and their tribal communities. Upon release, students who returned to their reservations often found themselves unable to readjust to everyday life in their families. For some, the psychological impact of institutionalization made reintegration problematic. For others, ten years of enforced training in Anglo-American language, diet, hygiene, dress, and occupational practices resulted in a sense of alienation from traditional reservation lifeways. The shared experience of institutional confinement itself became a powerful cultural bond between former students, particularly as children from various tribal groups formed close friendships and social ties in the large regional schools. Rather than wholesale cultural assimilation, these institutions cultivated and strengthened a sense of "American Indian" identity that transcended specific tribal affiliations. Thus, an unintended (and somewhat ironic) result of institutional confinement was the creation of a new spirit of pan-tribalism (Lomawaima 1994). This transformed ethnic awareness in turn helped reinvigorate the underlying struggle for racial equality as former students redefined themselves as both Indians and American citizens (Lindauer 1997; Hertzberg 1971).

By the 1920s, changing administrative and economic policies at the Bureau of Indian Affairs brought the Indian boarding school system under fresh scrutiny. Disparagement culminated in the Meriam Report of 1928, which criticized the entire system for failing health standards, insufficient diet, and poor attitudes toward the American Indian students and educators (Adams 1995). Over the next decade, Indian boarding schools were predominantly replaced by day schools established on reservation lands.

Institutional Confinement in the Twentieth Century

Before the twentieth century, both criminal justice and poverty relief were overwhelmingly administered on the municipal, county, and state levels of government. A gradual centralization of these duties and provisions began to emerge over the 1890s, with the federal government playing an increasingly active role. Before 1900, the bulk of federal crimes involved bank robbery, counterfeiting, or moonshining, the violation of national liquor tax laws (Friedman 1993). Over the Progressive Era of the early twentieth century, a dramatic expansion of national government powers occurred as Congress approved new legislation to establish federal jurisdiction over income tax regulation, liquor prohibition, prostitution, and interstate motor vehicle theft.

Gladiator Schools: The Federal Prison System

The growing number of federal crimes naturally resulted in a steadily increasing number of convicts. A subdivision of the Department of Justice, the Federal Prison System was created in 1891 when Congress authorized construction funds for penitentiaries at Fort Leavenworth, Kansas (1895), Atlanta, Georgia (1902), and McNeil Island, Puget Sound (1907). By 1930, when Congress established the Federal Bureau of Prisons in the Department of Justice, five federal prisons operated, including the Federal Industrial Institution for Women at Alderson, West Virginia (1927) (Friedman 1993: 269).

Leavenworth Penitentiary, the first federal prison to reach completion, was originally established in 1874 as a military prison for the U.S. Army. Transferred to the Department of Justice in the mid-1890s, the new penitentiary compound utilized a symmetrical neoclassical layout explicitly designed to intimidate (Bright 1996). Patterned after the Capitol building in Washington, D.C., and much unchanged today, the main facility consisted of two massive rectangular seven-story cell houses joined in the center by a rotunda surmounted by a grand dome. A monumental red brick wall still encloses the 22-acre penitentiary compound. Four feet thick, the original wall rose 35 feet above the ground and sank an additional 35 feet below ground to prevent diligent inmates from burrowing to freedom.

Each cell house consisted of two separate structures—a five-story block of adjoining rows of individual cells all encased within a massive stone facade. Narrow rectangular windows running the length of each cell house captured all the heat generated during the scorching Kansas summers. Functioning like a greenhouse, the cell house architecture actively contributed to the misery of incarceration. Inmate discomfort has not diminished over time as journalist Pete Earley, who from 1987 to 1989 interviewed Leavenworth inmates, makes clear:

> No one disagrees about the fifth tier. It is agony. The air is thick, hot to the tongue. Convicts sit on mattresses at night on the top tier as if in a narcotic stupor, naked except for sweat-soaked boxer shorts. They keep

their cells dark, afraid that the heat generated by the single 100-watt bulb above the metal sink will make the cell even more unbearable. Their bodies are covered with a thin layer of sweat that gleams even in the blackness when illuminated by the red glow of a half-spent cigarette. When you walk along the fifth tier you can smell the sweat and stale smoke. Sometimes, a face will loom forward from a darkened cell, appearing a ghostly white behind the inch-thick steel bars before disappearing moments late into the blackness. (1992: 29)

Currently in operation, Leavenworth serves as the largest maximum security prison in the United States, incarcerating approximately 2,000 inmates.

Alcatraz Island, the most infamous of federal penitentiaries, was originally established by the U.S. Army as part of its nineteenth-century coastal defense system. Located on a rocky outcrop inside San Francisco Bay, California, the isolated fort first served as a military prison during the Civil War. By the early twentieth century, changes in weapons technology made the brick and earthen fortifications obsolete, and Alcatraz was formally recommissioned in 1907 as the "United States Military Prison, Pacific Branch" (Odier 1982). To improve

Figure 2.5. Cell house and recreation yard, Alcatraz Island Federal Penitentiary, California. (Courtesy of Golden Gate National Recreational Area, Park Archives [GGNRA/PARC 82-C-17].)

security, construction of a three-story cell house of 600 cells was begun in 1909 (figure 2.5). When completed in 1912, this monumental penitentiary was acknowledged as the world's largest reinforced concrete structure. Similar to the interior design of Leavenworth Penitentiary, the four cell blocks inside the concrete facade were built as freestanding structures of steel and concrete. Additions also included a reinforced concrete lighthouse immediately south of the main entrance and a parade ground for the assembly and drilling of convicts on the western side of the island (National Park Service 1993).

By 1915, Alcatraz was the primary place of confinement for convicted soldiers stationed in the western United States, the Pacific, and the Panama Canal zone. Military convicts were assigned obsolete or condemned military uniforms rather than unique prison clothing. While cells were uncomfortable and the island a lonely place to be confined, the daily routine of scheduled assemblies and work assignments was not dramatically different from that of a regular garrison (Thompson 1979: 287–89). In addition to the main cell house, an electric power plant and laundry were installed between 1910 and 1912. Industrial buildings were constructed, with prisoners employed at blacksmithing, plumbing, and painting, as well as the manufacture of Army uniforms, gloves, hats, and shoes. Operating costs associated with the military prison remained high, particularly as the absence of a freshwater source on the isolated site necessitated the frequent provision and secure storage of water (Delgado 1991: 28). Concern over these expenses mounted steadily, and Alcatraz was transferred to the Bureau of Prisons in the Department of Justice in October 1933.

Designed for maximum security incarceration, the new federal penitentiary accommodated particularly notorious or dangerous criminals. Importantly, the Alcatraz penal regime demonstrated that the nature of incarceration had again transformed over the Progressive Era of the early twentieth century. In a stark departure from the optimistic philosophies of rehabilitation that had informed the construction of penitentiaries since the Jacksonian era, Alcatraz Island was established to enforce institutional confinement strictly as a mode of punishment. While productive labor was an important aspect of life on The Rock, prison industries now operated either as vocational training programs or to serve U.S. government contracts with military bases around the San Francisco Bay (figure 2.6). Thus, by the twentieth century, federal penitentiaries had evolved as subsidized institutions of the American state. Wider expectations of self-sustaining or even profit generating institutional economies remained abandoned until the reappearance of privatized prisons during the final decades of the century (Wacquant 2001; Mathiesen 1990).

Confining an average inmate population of 260, Alcatraz Federal Penitentiary was run according to a strict set of regulations that dictated the everyday

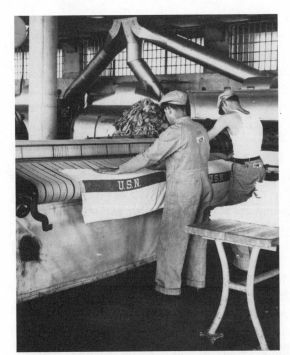

Figure 2.6. Inmates working on U.S. Navy laundry contract, Alcatraz Island Federal Penitentiary, California, ca. 1942. (Courtesy of Golden Gate National Recreational Area, Park Archives [GGNRA/PARC P77-C-34].)

Figure 2.7. Cell Block A, cell house, Alcatraz Island Federal Penitentiary, California. (Library of Congress, Historic American Buildings Survey-California [HABS CAL 38-ALCA, 1-A-17].)

lives of all inmates (figure 2.7). Despite its grim reputation as "Hellcatraz"—an island of the damned—living conditions were similar, if not better, than those at other federal penitentiaries. Inmates suffered no overcrowding, the cell house was maintained at a comfortable temperature of seventy degrees Fahrenheit, and after the mid-1950s cells were equipped with a headset that could be tuned into prison-run radio programs. Cell property, while strictly regulated, included a limited range of permissible toiletries and personal possessions (table 2.2). Bedding and clothing were frequently exchanged and cleaned in the prison laundry. Food, while bland and repetitive, was provided in plentiful quantities. Over its twenty-nine years of operation, Alcatraz Federal Penitentiary housed a total of 1,576 inmates, the vast majority of whom transferred to other lower security institutions after fulfilling their period of maximum security detention (Delgado 1991: 34).

The design and operation of federal prisons for women differed greatly. The first was established in 1927 at Alderson, West Virginia. Directed by Dr. Mary B. Harris, the Federal Industrial Institute for Women confined inmates in a series of barracks (or "cottages") located in a secure compound of 500 acres (Friedman 1993: 428). Intended for the incarceration of all female federal prisoners with sentences greater than twelve months, the prison trained inmates in domestic and office skills, farming, vegetable and fruit canning, and candy making. The comparatively relaxed security employed at Alderson reflected the fact that women tended to be convicted of drug and property offenses rather than violent crimes. Of the 505 inmates incarcerated in October 1935, "more than half (264) had been convicted of narcotics charges; there were 80 on liquor charges, 58 for counterfeiting and forgery, 18 for violating the Motor Vehicle Theft Act—and only one for homicide" (Friedman 1993: 429).

Crimes committed by women tended to violate state and municipal laws, resulting in far greater female populations in state prisons, where facilities varied dramatically, than in federal penitentiaries. The state prison at Bedford Hills in Westchester County, New York, utilized the "cottage plan" when it opened in 1900. Housed in barracks of twenty-eight rooms, inmates were each provided with a shared kitchen and flower garden and encouraged to participate in educational programs that included singing lessons and gymnastics. In stark contrast, before a separate women's building was added in 1927 to San Quentin State Prison in Marin County, California, women were confined in a "bear pit"—a cell building of 40 by 20 feet encased within an exclusion space of 60 by 90 feet. Incarcerating up to thirty women at a time, the structure provided neither heat nor indoor plumbing for toilets or showers (Friedman 1993: 428). No separate state facilities for female prisoners were established until the California Institution for Women opened at Tehachapi in the 1930s.

Table 2.2. Permitted Cell Property, U.S. Federal Penitentiary at Alcatraz Island

Cell issue equipment	Number
Shelves	2
Sheets stationery	2
Envelopes	2
Can cleanser	1
Pencils	3
Radio headset	1
Sink stopper	1
75-watt light bulb	1
Wall peg	4
Whisk broom	1
Lamp shade	1
Set "Institutional Regulations"	1
Rolls toilet paper	1
Drinking cup	1
Ashtray	1
Cleaning rags	2
Wastebasket	1
BEDDING	
Mattresses (maximum)	2
Blankets	1–4
Sheets	2
Pillows	2
Pillowcases (if 2 pillows)	2
TOILET ARTICLES	
Shaving cup	1
Razor blades	2
Safety razor	1
Cake soap	1
Comb	1
Pair nail clippers	1
Can toothpowder	1
Toothbrush	1
Shaving brush	1
Mirror	1
Face towel	1
Cake shaving soap	1

Source: Golden Gate National Park Association, "Institutional Rules and Regulations: United States Penitentiary, Alcatraz, California," Unpublished document (San Francisco: National Park Service, 1983), 9.

Note: The penitentiary rules include the caveat "No special shelves, boxes, desks or picture frames will be allowed."

Toward a New Deal for All: Social Welfare in the Early Twentieth Century

Over the early decades of the twentieth century, public welfare and assistance programs underwent a process of centralization similar to that of the criminal justice system. At the turn of the century, with the significant exception of federal jurisdiction over Native American communities, responsibilities for poor relief and education remained firmly situated either within the realms of state and municipal governments or in the hands of public philanthropic organizations such as the National Conference on Charities and Corrections. Nonetheless, the various and passionate national campaigns of the Progressive Era brought issues of workers' rights, childhood education, health and sanitation, alcoholism, and prostitution to the attention of Congress.

One particularly visible movement involved the establishment of quasi-institutional urban "settlement houses" by wealthy socialists and charity activists (Davis 1967). These welfare associations provided boardinghouse-style accommodation for the urban poor, encouraged the application of personal discipline, and offered daily routines designed for moral and educational improvement. Despite their adoption of these aspects of institutional life, the settlement houses operated more as benevolent community centers than as places of confinement. Offering a pragmatic response to the needs of the immigrant urban communities they served, the settlements taught English classes, sponsored art exhibits, fostered ethnic crafts, offered child care facilities for working mothers, and taught a range of occupational and domestic skills. While the most famous of the settlements was Hull House, established by Jane Addams on Halstead Street in Chicago (Addams 1910), over 400 of these institutions for mutual aid had been founded across cities of the Northeast and Midwest by 1910 (Katz 1986: 159).

With a widespread adoption of electric power over the early decades of the twentieth century, a frantic drive toward greater production, speed, and efficiency gripped American industrialization. Anxious to clear their factories of less productive or technologically redundant workers, business and government leaders created policies that both reorganized the workforce and shifted a growing number of groups into institutional forms of social management. Thus, the Progressive Era was marked by a "massive growth of institutions stretching all the way from schools and hospitals on one side to prisons and madhouses on the other"—a proliferation which further represented "not just the progress of medicine, education, or crime prevention, but the clearing of the marketplace of all but the 'economically active' and 'functioning' members of society" (Braverman 1974: 280). As the twin forces of foreign immigration and industrial expansion continued to produce increasing rates of urban poverty, municipal governments began to form collective bodies to develop shared solutions to welfare provision. In 1916, city boards of public welfare across the country combined to form the National Public Welfare League, headquartered in Kansas City (Katz 1986: 155).

This general trend toward centralization of government powers culminated in the New Deal era of the 1930s. By the summer of 1933, national unemployment rates had climbed to approximately 25 percent of the working population. Accepting the magnitude of deprivation facing Americans, President Franklin Delano Roosevelt set out to combat the Great Depression by recasting the federal government as a central instrument for social care and criminal management. Through his New Deal legislation and public works programs, Roosevelt transformed the fundamental structures of American capitalism:

> Emergency programs did prevent mass starvation and, very possibly, massive social disorder. Social security did introduce the idea of entitlement into national policy and establish federal responsibility for a wide range of human problems. Even more, the new legislation vastly augmented the scope of the national government, altered the very nature of federalism, and reorganized relations between the national state and its citizens. (Katz 1986: 208)

In addition to creating a nationalized system of social security insurance, Roosevelt established a massive program of federally funded civil works. By 1941, centrally managed organizations such as the Civilian Conservation Corp, the Work Projects Administration, the National Youth Administration, and the Civil Works Administration cast the federal government as a primary employer for Americans. Program participants were typically accommodated in residential centers, vocational boarding schools, or military-style barracks. To efficiently mobilize and coordinate the massive construction projects undertaken by these agencies, participants' work practices were strictly regimented and standardized. Thus, while strictly speaking not a mode of institutional confinement, these New Deal programs not only established a new relationship of paternalistic responsibility between the federal government and its citizens, but also established institutional modes of employment and accommodation as the standard for public programs.

Exile to Nowhere: Confinement and the Home Front in World War II

On December 7, 1941, Japanese forces bombed a U.S. naval base at Pearl Harbor, Hawaii, causing the United States to enter World War II. In the shock and confusion that followed the attack, long-standing racial prejudices rapidly surfaced across America, and people of Japanese ancestry living in California, Washington, and Oregon were faced with questions of national loyalty. On Feb-

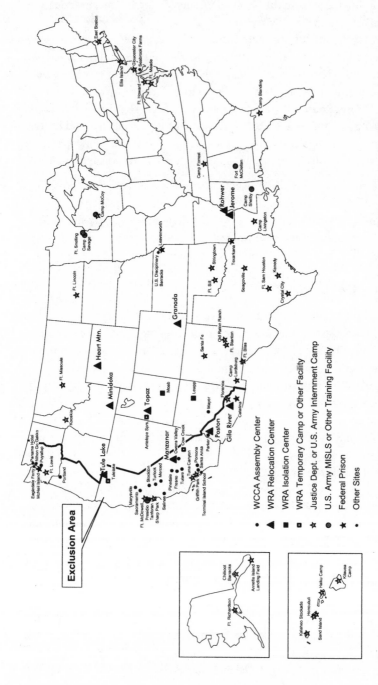

Figure 2.8. Sites in the United States associated with the relocation of Japanese-Americans during World War II. (Reproduced by permission of Jeffery F. Burton, Western Archaeological and Conservation Center, National Park Service.)

Figure 2.9. "Entrance to Manzanar, Manzanar Relocation Center," California, 1943. (Photograph by Ansel Adams. Library of Congress, Prints and Photographs Division [LC-DIG-ppprs-00286].)

ruary 19, 1942, Franklin Delano Roosevelt signed Executive Order No. 9066, permitting the U.S. Army to designate exclusion zones along the West Coast. From March through October 1942, approximately 120,000 men, women, and children of Japanese ancestry—two-thirds of whom were American citizens— were removed from their homes and confined in assembly camps, relocation centers, and prison camps without formal charges or trials (Farrell and Burton 2004: 22).

Built to house an average 10,000 internees each, the ten relocation centers established across eastern California, Arizona, Utah, Idaho, Wyoming, Colorado, and Arkansas (figure 2.8) were administered through the War Relocation Authority (WRA), a civilian organization created in March 1942 to help relieve the U.S. Army of noncombat operations (Daniels et al. 1991). Located in isolated regions, typically deserts or swamps, the relocation centers were designed to be self-contained facilities with hospitals, post offices, schools, warehouses, offices, factories, and residential areas all contained by a perimeter fence of barbed wire and secured by guard towers. Linked to the local highway by a single main entrance (figure 2.9) and intended to be as self-sufficient as possible, the main compound of each relocation center was surrounded by a large buffer zone used as farmland. To discourage fraternization, units of Military

Figure 2.10. "Mrs. Naguchi and two children, Manzanar Relocation Center," California, 1943. (Photograph by Ansel Adams. Library of Congress, Prints and Photographs Division [LC-DIG-ppprs-00246].)

Police assigned to the centers were provided with separate living quarters adjacent to the enclosed compounds, and civilian employees were usually housed in the nearby towns that served as supply centers.

Issues of order and containment, rather than surveillance, determined the architectural layout of relocation centers. Plans were arranged according to a rectilinear grid system of blocks that varied in size depending on the administrative or residential function of each zone. Internal access consisted of networks of unpaved dirt roads, which made the compounds either dusty or muddy places depending on the season. Each residential block consisted of ten to fourteen barracks, a mess hall, a laundry, a recreation hall, and separate latrines for men and women (Burton 1996: 29). Designed to offer semipermanent shelter, the barracks were constructed of weatherboard (figure 2.10). Internal wallboard was provided as insulation in colder climates, and roofs consisted of tarpaper-covered boards. Until "Mastipave" flooring (a linoleum substitute) was installed to insulate floors at some relocation centers, the internal raised wooden floors provided no barrier to the dust and dirt stirred up throughout the unpaved compounds.

Uniformly 20 feet wide by 120 feet long, individual barracks were internally divided into rooms of six standardized dimensions intended to accommodate

Table 2.3. Quartermaster Property Shipped to War Relocation Authority Relocation Centers, 1942

Item	Amount	Item	Amount
Axes	2,635	Pans, Cake or Pie	18,116
Blankets	275,141	Pans, Baking, large	2,894
Boats, Gravy	19,915	Pans, Frying	618
Bowls, Sugar	21,002	Picks, Ice	590
Bowls, Soup	123,583	Pins, Rolling	592
Buckets	9,478	Pitchers, Syrup	19,390
Cans, 10 gallon	4,159	Pitchers, Water	19,774
Cans, 32 gallon	5,555	Plates, Dinner	125,627
Cleavers	604	Platters, Meat	10,149
Cots, Steel	117,393	Pots, Mustard	19,879
Cups, Coffee	122,797	Pots, 10 gallon	1,292
Dippers	5,166	Pots, 15 gallon	1,340
Dishes, Vegetable	39,195	Pots, 20 gallon	466
Dishes, Pickle	10,125	Ranges, Army No. 5	1,236
Forks	117,620	Saucers, Coffee	123,345
Forks, Meat	2,434	Saws, Butcher	625
Graters	1,224	Scrapers, Dough	586
Griddles	1,240	Shakers, Salt	20,444
Knives, Paring	3,518	Shakers, Pepper	17,600
Knives	121,114	Sieves, Flour	594
Knives, Butcher	1,805	Skimmers	1,521
Ladles, Soup	3,518	Spoons	117,821
Machines, Grinder	659	Spoons, Basting	1,348
Mashers, Potato	1,207	Steels, Butcher	560
Mattress Covers	118,626	Tongs, Ice	639
Measures, Quart	1,207	Turners, Cake	2,507
Openers, Can	1,179	Whips, Wire	1,213
Pans, Dish	5,228		

Source: J. DeWitt, *Final Report, Japanese Evacuation from the West Coast, 1942* (Washington, D.C.: U.S. Government Printing Office, 1943), 276.

differently sized families and groups of single people. Since no ceilings were installed, the partition walls of each room extended only to the eaves of each room partition, leaving a crawl space between the walls and the boarded roof. Each apartment had a heating unit. Latrines were sex segregated and communal, with toilet stalls and bathtubs provided only in the women's facilities. All relocation centers were equipped with portable goods provided through the War Department, including communal kitchen equipment, dining ceramics, and apartment furnishings (table 2.3).

Following their confinement, internees continued to improve their center facilities by designing and constructing community buildings, including schools, churches, and cooperative stores. These structures were typically more individualistic in design than government buildings and utilized more permanent construction materials. The school buildings at Poston Relocation Center, for example, were built of adobe brick rather than weatherboard. Perhaps in subtle challenge to the institutionalization of their lives, internees tended to construct their later buildings at alternative angles to the uniform grid of the camp landscape (Burton 1996: 32).

As in the Indian boarding schools, expressions of ethnicity helped those confined cope with their institutional environment. Although the Japanese language was banned in the centers, Japanese writing adorned numerous concrete features outside the fenced central areas of camps. (For a detailed survey, see chapter 4.) This internee graffiti—inscribed onto stockade walls, concrete foundations, and local landscape monuments—typically utilized a combination of English and Japanese script (Inomata and Burton 1996; see also Burton et al. 1999). Memorials constructed in the cemeteries at Manzanar, Rohwer, and Granada, as well as individual headstones at most centers, tended to be marked with Japanese inscriptions (Burton et al. 2001). Numerous rice bowls, teacups, and sake bottles recovered during archaeological testing at the Manzanar Relocation Center demonstrate that interred families personalized their ceramics (Burton et al. 1999: 15–16). Internees landscaped their camps with gardens, ponds, irrigation systems, and stone features reflecting their Japanese heritage (figure 2.11). Through their material worlds, detained Japanese-Americans mediated the impact of institutional confinement by creating personalized spaces and markers of community identity.

Representing the largest single forced relocation in American history, the internment of Japanese-Americans brought a shameful new ambiguity to the question of civil rights due to national citizens. Unlike the incarceration of captured enemy soldiers during the Civil War, those confined in the relocation centers had never been convicted of any serious act of treason, espionage, or sabotage during the course of World War II (figure 2.12). Instead, Japanese-Americans volunteered in large numbers for U.S. military service. At almost every relocation center, internees built an honor roll monument inscribed with the names of servicemen from their community. While their families and communities waited out the war in the institutional confines of isolated camps, Japanese-American soldiers serving in the segregated combined unit of the 442nd Regimental Combat Team and the 100th Infantry Battalion of the Hawaii National Guard made it the most decorated unit of its size in American history (Uyeda 1995). Providing nearly 1,000 servicemen, the Minidoka camp in Idaho suffered the greatest number of casualties of all the Japanese-American relocation centers (Burton and Farrell 2001: 18).

Figure 2.11. Stela, Manzanar Relocation Center, California, 2003. (Reproduced by permission of Jeffery F. Burton, Western Archaeological and Conservation Center, National Park Service.)

Figure 2.12. "Roy Takano at a town hall meeting, Manzanar Relocation Center," California, 1943. (Photograph by Ansel Adams. Library of Congress, Prints and Photographs Division [LC-DIG-ppprs-00374].)

Further, in contrast with the Indian boarding school system, those subjected to WRA confinement did not draw upon government-funded entitlements or support programs before their incarceration. By the time the last internees were released during 1946, Japanese-Americans had lost homes and businesses later estimated to be worth (in today's values) at least four billion dollars (Farrell and Burton 2004: 22). The federal government had simply assumed the power to incarcerate a racially defined group of Americans who were neither criminal nor perceived as financially dependent. On December 18, 1944, in the landmark case *Korematsu v. United States*, the Supreme Court upheld this extraordinary expansion of federal power on the grounds of "military necessity" (Burton 1996: 43). Did the ideals of the New Republic retain any relevance by the twentieth century? Could institutional confinement be considered a method of rehabilitation—a social instrument linked to late eighteenth-century republican ideologies of citizenship, liberty, and civil rights (Rothman 1990)? Or had it evolved into a sinister, if not capricious, expression of the state's power over those considered unproductive, dangerous, or merely different?

A War for National Security: The Future of American Institutional Confinement

Profound debates over citizenship and human rights continue to haunt the American experience of institutional confinement in the first decade of the twenty-first century. Following the terrorist attacks of September 11, 2001, the United States led a multinational force into conflict in Afghanistan. Intending to destabilize the Al-Qaeda network of loosely affiliated terrorists and capture its primary financier Osama bin Laden, American-led forces began to inter captured enemy fighters at the U.S. Naval Base at Guantánamo Bay, Cuba. With the invasion of Iraq during April 2003, the population of detainees continued to grow. Two years later, approximately 550 inmates, representing more than thirty nationalities, remain incarcerated at Guantánamo Bay without formal charges or trial (Amnesty International 2005a).

Described by former U.S. secretary of defense, Donald Rumsfeld, as "among the most dangerous, best-trained vicious killers on the face of the earth," (U.S. DoD 2002) these detainees have been identified as "enemy combatants" and therefore exempt from the international treaties that establish minimum standards of rights and entitlements for those captured during wartime. Confined in solitary isolation in the maximum security blocks of Camp Delta, these detainees have been denied access to legal representation and external monitoring during military interrogations. Those released, including four British nationals repatriated and released without charges in January 2005, have claimed they experienced serious abuses of their human rights and suffered deteriorating mental health as a result of their incarceration (BBC 2005a; BBC 2005b).

By August 2005, a fluctuating number of detainees initiated a hunger strike to protest the general conditions of their incarceration and their continued detention without trial. Nearly five months later, with eighty-four detainees refusing food, a Guantánamo spokesman admitted the U.S. Army provided "appropriate nutrition through nasal tubes"—a process defined as force feeding by the United Nations (BBC 2005c). In February 2006, a United Nations draft report concluded that involuntary feeding, in addition to "several interrogation techniques such as prolonged solitary confinement, and exposure to extreme temperatures, noise and light," created conditions of incarceration that "in several areas violates international law and conventions on human rights and torture" (BBC 2006). The report ultimately advised closure of the Guantánamo Bay facility. On May 18, 2006, a violent uprising struck the compound when inmates, using handheld weapons fashioned from sticks, lights, and fan components, clashed with guards (Goldenberg and Walsh 2006: 20). With approximately thirty-nine suicide attempts documented since 2003, human rights officials claimed the incident reflected growing despair within the detainee population.

Various other foreign governments and international bodies—including the International Committee of the Red Cross (ICRC) and Amnesty International—have questioned the right of the United States government to contravene the Third Geneva Convention. In response to the genocidal atrocities that accompanied World War II, the four Geneva Conventions were approved by international treaty during August 1949 to govern both the protection of civilian populations and the conduct of hostilities during wartime (ICRC 2005). The Third Geneva Convention guarantees minimum humanitarian standards of treatment for prisoners of war. Underlying debates over conditions at Camp Delta focus on the legality of confinement. By defining inmates as enemy combatants, were the Guantánamo Bay detainees exempt from treaty requirements established for prisoners of war?

With the transfer of Jose Padilla (or Abdullah al Muhajir) from Justice Department custody to military control on June 9, 2002, ambiguities of citizenship and civil rights once again plague the American experience of institutional confinement. On May 8, 2002, Padilla was arrested after landing at Chicago's O'Hare International Airport, having returned from Pakistan on what authorities determined was a "reconnaissance mission" for the Al-Qaeda terrorist network (BBC 2002). An American citizen with an extensive criminal record, Padilla allegedly converted to Islam while serving a jail sentence in the mid-1990s and had plotted to detonate a dirty bomb in an unspecified American city. Following his transfer to military jurisdiction, Padilla has been detained for an indefinite period with neither official charges nor access to an attorney (R. A. Levy 2003). A number of public policy organizations—including the Center for National Security Studies, the Lawyers Committee for Human Rights, the Cato Institute, and the Rutherford Institute—have become involved in legal debates surrounding this case, arguing that the detention of Padilla represents a clear infringement of his constitutional rights. Despite the Bush administration's designation of Padilla as an enemy combatant, these organizations contend that as an American citizen, Padilla retains the right to protection against deprivation of liberty without "due process of law" as guaranteed by the Fifth Amendment. He holds additional rights to information on the nature and cause of charges, to formal legal representation, and to a "speedy and public trial" as elaborated in the Sixth Amendment (R. A. Levy 2003).

Six decades after Japanese-Americans were interred without charges or trial, "military necessity" has once again been invoked to justify the indefinite detention of an American citizen without due legal process. The national experience of institutional confinement thus continues to generate passionate debate over the philosophical basis and humanitarian consequences of incarceration. As his case moves through the judicial system, Jose Padilla remains a symbol of the enduring ambiguities that surround American citizenship and the experience of incarceration. The next chapter will examine these theoretical debates by presenting the central models of power relations that have framed archaeological studies of institutional confinement.

Why Incarcerate?

Why confine people within an institution? How do institutions operate? What wider social, political, or economic purposes are served by institutional confinement? This chapter will consider four broadly defined theoretical models to demonstrate how the experience of institutional confinement articulates with the wider constitution of American society. For the purposes of this overview, these approaches have variously interrogated the institutional dynamics of punishment, reform, and deterrence; domination and resistance; reform, respite, and ritual; and coping, survival, and exchange.

As discussed in the last chapter, the increasingly professionalized character of institutional services after the Civil War produced a steadily growing array of philosophical and clinical fields devoted to the study (if not the perfection) of institutional confinement. Today, a thriving range of social and medical sciences share overlapping spheres of concern with various types of institutions. Penal confinement, for example, is variously explored through "criminology" (patterns of crime in American society or what makes citizens offend), "penology" (interior operations of prisons and their wider role in society), and "penality" (the sociology of penal policies or how prisons work on inmates and staff). Similarly, while pedagogy examines the roles and functions of educational institutions, both sociology and social work consider the impact of institutional confinement as a method of poverty management. Finally, an array of specialized medical disciplines, such as psychiatry, psychology, and clinical psychotherapy, focus on the treatment of mental illnesses through institutional modes of care.

These various social sciences ultimately consider how institutions produce the social roles embodied in the familiar characters that inhabit places of confinement—inmate, guard, administrator, volunteer, doctor, teacher, student, and patient. How do these diverse inhabitants experience the institution? What forges the relationships of solidarity, hostility, or indifference that in turn shape alliances between those who incarcerate and those who are incarcerated? By exploring the power relations inherent to this unique form of social management, scholars from these specialist fields actually examine the operation of power itself.

But what is power? Recognized as a social relationship, power was classically defined by Max Weber as "the probability that one actor within a social relationship will be in a position to carry out his own will despite resistance" (1947: 152). More recent studies have diversified Weber's basic definition. Daniel Miller and Christopher Tilley (1984) distinguish two primary forms of power: "power over" others, defined as acts of domination, and "power to" act, defined as resistance. Eric Wolf suggests four operational hierarchies of power: the personal, interpersonal, organizational, and the overarching political-economic (1990). Others draw from interdisciplinary models that conceive of power as subjective performances or practices (Butler 1993) or explain the way such social practices are simultaneously enabled and constrained by the wider structures of society (Giddens 1984; Bourdieu 1977). Finally, with a growing number of archaeologists noting that power rarely manifests as a uniform hierarchy of imposed will, an interest in the internal dynamics of power has emerged through our scholarly literature (see O'Donovan 2002 and J. E. Levy 1999). Many of these investigations adopt the concept of heterarchy and explore the dynamics of factionalism as dialectical or counterpoised modes of power are shared and traded between different social groups (Gero 2000; Spencer-Wood 1999; Marquardt 1992; Crumley 1987).

This chapter will similarly consider particular material expressions of power created by places of confinement. Further, and perhaps more significantly, it will explore the limits of power by interrogating the means by which inhabitants negotiate, modify, and survive the process of institutionalization. As observed in chapter 1, this archaeological approach offers both functionalist and experiential perspectives on power by illuminating both how it physically operates on institutional inhabitants and also how these material practices shape the broader experiences and understandings of diverse occupants. To enter into what promise to be enduring debates, we will first consider classic theoretical explanations of the modern institution.

Punishment, Reform, and Deterrence

Traditional debates over correctional reform have long queried the basic function of institutional confinement. Why does the state detain populations of its citizens? According to traditional criminological approaches, the underlying intention is to effect a triangulated combination of punishment, deterrence, and reform upon the inmate. Within this basic tripartite framework, scholars and practitioners have passionately argued over the relative merits of these three basic aims. Each philosophical stance has offered some recipe of one or more of these aims as the "true" function of institutional confinement. These

Figure 3.1. Triangular map of classic criminological debates.

specific positions can be relationally mapped within a conceptual triangular diagram (figure 3.1).

The Right of Punishment

Early criminological debates considered the relationship between punishment and the constitution of society. In constructing his humanistic vision of enlightened governance, Immanuel Kant argued that a transgression of public law, or crime, rendered the subject incapable of being a citizen. Further, the right to administer punishment was invested in the sovereign as the head of state. For Kant, who likened ideas of reform to perilous medical experimentation, the absolute justice of punishment provided a sublime goal in and of itself:

> For if justice and righteousness perish, human life would no longer have any value in the world. What, then, is to be said of such a proposal as to keep a criminal alive who has been condemned to death, on his being given to understand that if he agreed to certain dangerous experiments being performed upon him, he would be allowed to survive if he came happily through them? . . . [A] court of justice would repudiate with scorn any proposal of this kind if made to it by the medical faculty; for

justice would cease to be justice, if it were bartered away for any consideration whatever. (Kant 1887: 195–96)

Similarly, Georg Wilhelm Friedrich Hegel dismissed concepts of deterrence or reform as irrelevant, claiming that the state had a duty to vindicate the "abstract rationality of the individual's volition":

> Punishment is regarded as containing the criminal's right and hence by being punished he is honoured as a rational being. He does not receive this due of honour unless the concept and measure of his punishment are derived from his own act. Still less does he receive it if he is treated either as a harmful animal who has to be made harmless, or with a view to deterring and reforming him. (Hegel 1969: 100)

In these early assessments, punishment is required as an expression of accountability—a gesture of recognition and respect due the citizen inmate.

This traditional focus where reason and accountability inform the role of punishment has been characterized as "retributivist" (or vindictive) theory. Retributivist theory emphasizes a *moral* improvement of the world as a result of punishment (Ezorsky 1972: xviii). Alternatively, scholars such as Emile Durkheim consider the positive effect of punishment as an essentially *social* phenomenon. In Durkheim's model (1964), punishment operates as a profound social necessity because it serves to uphold underlying structures, thereby preventing the gradual erosion and collapse of human societies. For Durkheim, "the moral (or mental) aspects and the social (or material) aspects of group life" are mutually constitutive (Garland 1990: 24). Under normal conditions, these two aspects operate together as different dimensions of a cohesive social whole. In other words, all human societies require a moral framework, as even the most basic exchange between individuals demands an accepted set of norms (or collective representations) for the encounter to occur. At the same time, this moral framework reflects the underlying social organization that bonds people to each other.

Punishment therefore offers more than a simple instrument of crime control. In Durkheim's view, it exists to ensure social solidarity—to support collectively held sentiments. Punishment provides an occasion for the collective demonstration of the shared ethical framework and, through that very act of communal expression, a strengthening of the moral order itself. Punishments (including institutional confinement) offer "a sign that the authorities are in control, that crime is an aberration and that the conventions which govern social life retain their force and vitality" (Garland 1990: 59). Thus, according to this anthropologically influenced model, punishment operates more as a form of governance than as one of subgroup management. Determining the viability and moral character of a social group, allowing for the general maintenance of a social system, it constitutes crime by defining what is criminal and, in this process, constitutes society itself.

Reform

Alternatively, other scholars and professionals have answered the question "why confine?" by promoting the reformative capabilities incarceration offers. From the mid-eighteenth century, fervent advocates of reform shaped the design and operation of institutions across Great Britain and its global colonies. Penal reformers such as William Blackburn, John Howard, and John Jebb politically championed the moral and economic value of erecting institutions for the improvement and rehabilitation of criminals. Jonas Hanway similarly indulged his reformist principles by founding the first Magdalen Hospital in London during 1758, intending this establishment as a place where "unfortunate women could find an asylum and the chance to earn a respectable living" (Semple 1993: 84). As discussed in the previous chapter, Jeremy Bentham's institutional designs established a new materialist and particularly influential approach to the imposition of disciplinary reform (Semple 1993; Foucault 1977). Encapsulating offenders within individual cells, his ideal Panopticon exacted reform upon the criminal body through technologies of solitary isolation, religious education, and perpetual surveillance (Bentham 1791; see also figure 2.2).

By the early nineteenth century, a yearning for philanthropic improvement had spread across the Atlantic. This general desire to protect and enrich members of the "lower orders" drove groups of American citizens to found private charities and support publicly funded institutions dedicated to the reform of the indigent, disabled, and criminal. Enacted through principles of industry, parsimony, domestic ritual, and personal discipline, reformist ideologies influenced a generation of early nineteenth-century institutional designs (Garman 2005; De Cunzo 1995; Friedman 1993; Upton 1992; Dobash et al. 1986; Evans 1982; Freedman 1981). Fierce philosophical debates raged throughout the 1830s between proponents of the Auburn or congregate system and those who supported the Pennsylvania or separate system. Detailed in chapter 2, these two philosophies informed competing architectural models for the administration of reform. But despite passionate debate over their relative merits, both of these infamous American templates adopted regimentation and labor as essential mechanisms for cultivating improvement of the mortal soul (Dix 1845; see also Garman 1999; Rothman 1990).

By the second half of the century, economic and logistic issues had compromised these idealized progressive models of reform. Disgusted by what he perceived as the "measuring out of pains in order to meet some notion of impossible justice," late nineteenth-century penal activist Zebulon Brockway devised a fresh philosophical template for a new "American reformatory prison system" (1910). Drawing upon optimistic principles of practical reform, Brockway founded New York's Elmira Reformatory in 1877 as an institution for younger offenders deemed "malleable under the simultaneous reciprocal play of scientifically directed bodily and mental exercises." His previous experience in prison administration had demonstrated the ineffectiveness of deterrence as a central goal of institutional confinement. Far from feeling social disgrace or shame as a result of their incarceration, Brockway found that inmates developed a sense of self-importance triggered, in his opinion, by the corrupting influences of the legal, media, and peer attention showered upon them.

Brockway's emphasis on reform as a structuring principle of institutional confinement was intended to generate a sense of mutuality and interdependency within and among prisoners, thereby nurturing emotive links to wider American society. When combined with practical mechanisms for self-improvement, humane sensibilities would empower the inmate to fully reintegrate as a legitimate industrial worker. Most significantly, Brockway's reformatory approach advocated the concept of an "indeterminate sentence" as a method of ensuring true rehabilitation. In theory the duration of confinement would be determined by the inmate's speed of transformation, with confinement continued until either reformation occurred or the prisoner died without achieving release. Practice was another thing entirely: states that adopted Brockway's philosophy of reform soon compromised his model by introducing minimum sentencing laws and parole conditions (Friedman 1993: 160–61).

More recently, late twentieth-century attempts at reform have also emphasized the need for inmate and staff support, citing in particular the inadequate provision of drug treatment, violence management, medical care, and mental health programs in places of confinement (Kupers 1999; Owen 1998; Haney 1997; Prendergast et al. 1995; Fleisher 1989; Lombardo 1989). Recent work on rehabilitation schemes has acknowledged the fundamental racial and economic dynamics that produced strategies of mass confinement during the final decades of the twentieth century (Wacquant 2001; Mathiesen 1990; Katz 1986). At the start of the twenty-first century, technologies of infrastructural support that guide modern reformative confinement dovetail with the changing socioeconomic demands of the American industrial market and the increasing professionalization of specialist trades associated with institutional reform—a fact not lost on those who champion the aim of deterrence as a primary aim of institutional confinement.

Deterrence

Scholars in a third theoretical camp critique the entire concept of penal reform as a "dangerous myth" perpetuated by professional groups associated with modern institutions (Martinson 1972). These advocates observe that despite the best efforts of prison chaplains, correctional officers, teachers, vocational instructors, counselors, and psychiatrists, the carceral nature of wider society ultimately prevents the full rehabilitation and social reintegration of institutional inmates. In other words, the acute physical, emotional, and economic scars left by the experience of institutionalization prevent the inmate from ever escaping the general stigma of confinement. Even after release, where does one go, as an ex-inmate, to restart a civilian life? How does one hide their past from neighbors, relatives, communities, or potential employers?

Thus, for members of this third philosophical school, institutional confinement is primarily an effective means of social defense. Undertaken to incapacitate offensive behaviors, it is meant to protect society from various forms of otherness (such as crime, poverty, and racial or political heterogeneity) in the community of citizens. Confinement serves as a form of deterrence on an individual level by removing and neutralizing the deviant himself and on a corporate level by providing a terrible example of the consequences of deviant action.

Many scholars in this group adopt an explicitly materialist political and economic framework for their interpretation of institutional confinement. As first argued in 1931 by the Marxist scholar Georg Rusche, the prison is essentially created by wider social forms (Rusche and Kirchheimer 1968). Rusche employed two simple economic axioms to demonstrate the underlying social functions of crime and of institutional forms of confinement. The first axiom or "principle of less eligibility" posits that for institutional sanctions to properly operate as a deterrent, the conditions of confinement must be worse than the living conditions experienced by the lowest strata of the proletarian class (Rusche 1978). The second axiom states that the nature of punishment correlates with the state of the labor market. In other words, in societies where workers are scarce, institutional confinement is required to deter sloth—to make the unwilling work. Conversely, when a large reserve of potential workers is present, punishment no longer serves as a mode of labor exploitation. Harsh corporal and capital punishments are instead marshaled by the state to deter crime and poverty. The function of institutional confinement, according to this classic Marxist model, is essentially linked to the economic value of the offender's labor. Thus, by associating the emergence of institutional confinement with the consolidation of bourgeois power in Western state-based societies, Rusche offered a fresh historic analysis of confinement that explicitly connected types of punishment with different phases of capitalist modes of production (Howe 1994: 12–18; Garland 1990: 98–105).

Later revisions of the Rusche-Kirchheimer model refined it by revealing demographic correlations between institutional population rates and wider international patterns of unemployment (Findlay and Hogg 1988; Box 1987). One classic reinterpretation by the Italian Marxist scholars Dario Melossi and Massimo Pavarini (1981) demonstrates how oscillations in the ideological moral climate of a society—its general degree of enthusiasm for institutional detention—correspond with periods of economic expansion and recession. In his archaeological study of Rhode Island's nineteenth-century state prison, James Garman (2005) similarly interprets in the excavated architectural layout of his site a profound tension between overarching desires for parsimonious financial expenditure—represented by industrialized modes of convict labor in the prison workshops—and haphazard interests in philanthropic reform—represented in the design of inmate accommodation. Other scholars have taken a more critical view of the deterministic tendencies of the Rusche-Kirchheimer economic model, noting that the emergence of welfare-oriented and therapeutic forms of punishment in modern society complicate a purely functionalist study of social control (Katz 1986; Spitzer 1979).

Additionally, feminist scholars have argued for greater sensitivity to gendered patterns in the labor market, observing in particular the general invisibility of domestic and service-related employment in the Marxist studies. Citing statistical analyses demonstrating that women's imprisonment actually *decreases* during periods of economic crisis (while men's simultaneously increases), Adrian Howe suggests that working-class women, who are typically held responsible for family maintenance, are therefore even *less* likely to be incarcerated during periods of economic recession (1994: 42). Finally, since institutional confinement has not actually produced reformed workers, other scholars suggest that its primary purpose is to mobilize deterrence through the broader threat of stigmatization (Ferrajoli and Zolo 1985).

Ultimately, by exploring the philosophical dilemma of "the right to punish" (Garland 1983: 85), traditional approaches to the sociology of institutional confinement—retributive, reformative, and deterrent—have connected fundamental issues of the power to punish with wider questions about the moral, political, and economic constitution of American society. While various scholars have located the underlying value or aim of confinement in some combination of punishment, reform, and deterrence, enduring philosophical debate has encouraged a detailed appreciation of the moral basis of detention and its role in American social life. Further, by interrogating the socioeconomic frameworks that determine the subjects of incarceration and confinement, the traditional perspectives have illuminated the tangible material effects of institutionalization. They have demonstrated the pivotal role of confinement in the construction of relations between the American state and the American people (Garland 1990).

The Docile Inmate: On Domination and Resistance

Despite the volume of richly detailed work produced through penological and materialist studies, underlying social questions remain unanswered. Why does the state confine segments of its population? How does confinement operate on these subjects? How does it serve to mobilize social control? What does it mean to exact reform? How do those confined respond to their carceral experiences? Drawing from anthropological, sociological, legal, and historical studies, the multidisciplinary field of penality emerged as a means for exploring the social and ideological operation (or function) of power in the modern institution.

On the Production of Social Control

In her ethnographic studies of ritual order and symbolic contaminations, Mary Douglas (1966) defined power as the ability of a society to impose a system of symbolic classification on the surrounding natural world:

> Cultural categories are public matters. They cannot so easily be subject to revision. Yet they cannot neglect the challenge of aberrant forms. Any given system of classification must give rise to anomalies, and any given culture must confront events which seem to defy its assumptions. It cannot ignore the anomalies which its scheme produces, except at risk of forfeiting confidence. This is why, I suggest, we find in any culture worthy of the name various provisions for dealing with ambiguous or anomalous events. (40)

To sustain social order, cultures impose a judgmental and carefully partitioned schema on the surrounding world. Intended to neutralize ambiguous or anomalous events, this ideological schema keeps a culture's pure, clean, disciplined, docile, productive, and socialized elements safely distant from its contaminated, dirty, raw, refractory, unproductive, and natural elements. Active transgression of these elemental boundaries, identified as aberrant or criminal behavior, threatens a society by confronting its formative cultural logic and thereby challenging its basic legitimacy (Stoler 1995; McClintock 1995; Stallybrass and White 1986).

But how are cultural schemas introduced and maintained? How does the state impose such ideological constructs on its populations? Forced compliance, while a dramatic mode of enforcing respect and imposing will, does not offer a productive strategy for social control in the long term. When a state uses coercion, it "virtually inoculates the complier against willing compliance" (Scott 1990: 108). Not only failing to produce attitudes that would sustain compliance in the absence of force, state coercion in fact produces sharp reactions *against* those very attitudes.

Thus, only when compliance is generally perceived as voluntary or freely chosen can those in power effectively nurture compliant attitudes in those they lead. Investigating the power relations between citizenry and state, a notable company of sociologists, criminologists, penal historians, and social philosophers recognize the modern institution as the primary technology for establishing internalized and voluntary social acquiescence in human groups (see Garland 1990; Carlen 1983; Evans 1982; Ignatieff 1978; and Goffman 1961). For these scholars, institutional confinement, by virtue of its role as both an exclusive and intrusive form of accommodation, produces compliance by dominating or wielding "power over" its inhabitants.

Domination: An Architecture of the Mind

Louis Althusser offers a compelling Marxist interpretation of social exclusion, revealing the role of political and ideological strategies in the reproduction of power (1971, 1984). According to Althusser, relations of domination are authenticated and naturalized through the ideological apparatus to which people are born. These ideologies consist of belief and value systems accepted by the subordinate group as both valid and "common sense." Serving ultimately to mask the innate inequalities of the social system, these "dominant ideologies" operate by systematically promoting the interests of the controlling group. Through social interaction, people reproduce the dominant ideology. Further, the unequal apparatus becomes legitimated through social institutions, including the police, law courts, religious organizations, trade unions, and state bureaucracies.

In his revisionist studies, Michel Foucault offered a sophisticated reinterpretation of this explicitly Marxist approach to domination. His famous philosophical treatise *Discipline and Punish* (1977) traces radical transformations in the form of European and American punishment between the 1750s, when the public spectacle of torture dominated, and the 1830s, when disciplinary confinement emerged as the primary mode of punishment for the modern industrial state. While historical aspects of this study are discussed in chapter 2, the philosophical framework of Foucault's model offered such revolutionary insight on the internal dynamics of institutional confinement that separate consideration is warranted.

For Foucault, the very materiality of the prison serves as both an instrument and vector of power. As a technology for effecting power, the prison creates a "non-corporeal penality" (15). In other words, by subjecting the inmate's body to certain material experiences, disciplinary reform becomes enforced "on the heart, the thoughts, the will, the inclinations" of the prisoner (17). Linking the "birth" of the prison to preexisting sites of disciplinary power—armies, monasteries, schools, workshops—he argues that these institutional forms all share a "coercive, corporal, solitary, secret model of the power to punish" (131), which ultimately produces "subjected and practised bodies," or "docile bodies" through techniques of corrective training (138).

Within institutions, discipline is deployed as a "cluster of procedures" (Howe 1994: 92) for controlling individual inhabitants: surveillance, classification, routines, and examinations. Specific material techniques—such as solitary confinement, reinscription of personal identity (through institutional uniforms, haircuts, names, and badges), and routinized activity (repetitive taskwork, drills, parades, and musters)—exact an ideological reformation of deviant and transgressive behavior through the voluntary compliance of the inmate. These disciplinary techniques ultimately serve to "soften the mind to virtuous suggestion" (Ignatieff 1978: 74).

Extending the penal philosophies behind Jeremy Bentham's eighteenth-century Panopticon (figure 2.2), Foucault observes that the underlying significance of this unique architectural design lay in its basic function as a far more generalized mode of repressive power. Its institutional apparatus served to not only reform prisoners but also treat patients, instruct school children, confine the insane, supervise workers, and enforce industry upon the unproductive—to transform these various classes of non-compliant, delinquent, and marginalized inmates into malleable citizens of the state.

Foucault's radical reinterpretation of the prison inverts Rusche and Kirchheimer's first axiom of deterrence. Rather than arguing, as they do, that the prison is created by wider social forms, Foucault insists that wider social forms are essentially created by institutional confinement:

> Is it surprising that the cellular prison, with its regular chronologies, forced labour, its authorities of surveillance and registration, its experts in normality, who continue and multiply the functions of the judge, should have become the modern instrument of penality? Is it surprising that prisons resemble factories, schools, barracks, hospitals, which all resemble prisons? (227–28)

By inverting this traditional penological axiom, Foucault's analysis transcends existing (and rather stagnant) debate over the relative merits and failures of

punishment, reform, and deterrence. Noting that "the principle of penal detention has never seriously been questioned," Foucault instead asserts that the
carceral system itself provides "very precise functions" (272). By maintaining
delinquency, encouraging recidivism, and transforming the occasional offender into a habitual deviant, institutional confinement ultimately serves to
distinguish, classify, contain, and thereby neutralize those very aberrant (and
criminalized) behaviors that threaten the legitimacy of the state. Confinement
thus produces the basic modes of domination necessary for the maintenance
of American society.

How do disciplinary techniques actually operate upon the inmate? Sociological studies of institutional confinement have explored both the specific
modes of domination that function within institutions and their resulting impact on various types of inmate populations (see Carroll 1997; B. Foster et al.
1995; Rafter 1990; Carlen 1983; Sykes 1958; Stanton and Schwartz 1954; Cohen
1954). Within this literature, Erving Goffman's classic study of the "total institution" (1961) offers a detailed description of four primary conditions of institutionalization to which inmates must adapt regardless of their particular type of
confinement.

In Goffman's analysis, the first condition of institutionalization involves
mortification—or structured humiliation—of the inmate's sense of self. On
first entering prison, the inmate is subjected to an admissions procedure,
which operates as a form of initiation into the institutional world. Goffman
characterizes this initiation as a practice of "leaving off and taking on," marked
at midpoint by a moment of physical nakedness (18). Significantly, this mortification involves a ritual of material exchange: "leaving off" entails one's dispossession of all personal property and its subsequent replacement with substitute
belongings clearly marked as owned by the institution. The inmate's state of
material dispossession is further emphasized by regular search and seizure
events, during which all accumulated forms of property are recalled by institutional staff to be "disinfected of identifications" (19). The inmate undergoes
further mortification through the institution's withdrawal of objects associated
with his usual outward appearance. Denied unrestricted access to the accoutre-
ments of personal fashion and hygiene—clothes, brushes, cosmetics, towels,
soap, shaving sets, and bathing facilities—the inmate, stripped of his or her
familiar appearance, suffers a defacement of self-identity. As Goffman points
out, institutional substitutes are depersonalized, "typically of a 'coarse' variety,
ill-suited, often old, and the same for large categories of inmates" (20).

The second stage of institutional domination involves the production of a
"reassembled" inmate identity (De Cunzo 2006: 167). This secondary process
is enacted through the prisoner's formal and informal instruction in the privi-

lege system, which provides a framework for a new "personal reorganization" or institutional sense of self (Goffman 1961: 48). The inmate must learn three things in order to be reassembled within the institution: the formal "house rules" (or those regulations that choreograph the austere pattern of daily life); the rewards available for obedience (primarily consisting of minor privileges artificially elevated to great significance within the institution); and the punishments consequent to breaking institutional rules (Goffman 1961: 48–53).

Both the third and fourth conditions of inmate life require a familiarity with the institutional system. "Messing up" involves a complicated process of participating in forbidden activities, getting caught, and enduring the full weight of sanctions (Goffman 1961: 53–54). Providing a route into inmate subculture, "messing up," according to Goffman, serves both as a mechanism for redistributing power and privileges among inmates and as a means of inmate mobility. (Punishments of demotion mix institutional old-timers with newcomers and widen the exchange of insider information and illicit resources.) Such institutional connections in turn drive the final condition of institutional adaptation or "secondary adjustments" (Goffman 1961: 54). As inmates learn how to manipulate the system to their advantage, they develop an essential and intimate awareness of the limits of domination within the institution.

Despite the disciplinary weight of Goffman's "total institution," not all inmates yield to institutional domination. Since power exists both as forces of compliance and forces of action, resistance is born at the same moment as domination. Increasingly, social theorists are questioning the pervasiveness of dominant ideologies. As sociologist Anthony Giddens argues, "all social actors, no matter how lowly, have some degree of penetration of the social forms which oppress them" (1979: 72). Feminist critiques of Foucault's analysis of modern penal discipline particularly note the almost complete absence of human volition and consciousness in his discussion; in Foucault's discourse the prisoner is less an institutionally dominated being than a cog in the sociocarceral machine (Howe 1994; Butler and Scott 1992; Hartsock 1990). Do all institutional inmates become docile bodies? Can inmates evolve alternative modes of power? How would such modes operate? From an archaeological perspective, how would we materially recognize them?

Resistance: The Hidden Transcript

Ongoing elaborations of Antonia Gramsci's theory of cultural hegemony offer a view of power relations alternative to those where a passive subordinate is forced by compelling ideology to submit absolutely to the dominant institutional world. The term "hegemony" has been adopted by various scholars to refer to power as a fluidly shifting negotiation rather than as something possessed at the expense of others (Hebdige 1988; R. Williams 1977; Gramsci 1971). Essentially unstable, "hegemony is realized through the balancing of competing forces, not the crushing calculus of class domination" (Comaroff and Comaroff 1991: 20). Operating as a "prevailing consciousness," (Beaudry et al. 1991: 156), hegemony creates a "war of positions" (Miller et al. 1989: 11), that in turn nurtures alternative social bonds, allegiances, and consciousness.

Many scholars use the term "resistance" to refer to this alternative, negotiatory form of power. Despite his focus on the exercise of domination, Foucault also recognized the mutual existence of both modes: "Where there is power, there is resistance, and yet, or rather consequently, this resistance is never in a position of exteriority in relation to power" (1980: 95). Building upon this concept of mutuality, James Scott explores the origins, nature, and mobilization of resistance as an everyday expression of power designed to thwart systems of domination. His ethnographic work suggests that a desire for resistance originates in the mortifications of domination itself. In other words, the social experience of disgrace, submission, humiliation, forced deference, and punishment—the very negation of personal dignity imposed by institutional confinement—generates a "seedbed of the anger, indignation, frustration and swallowed bile" that in turn nurtures a yearning for alternatives (Scott 1990: 111).

Defining resistance as a constellation of activities intended to undermine, thwart, or obstruct conditions of domination, Scott contrasts resistance, as a form of subordinate power, with outright rebellion. Often subtle and anonymous, resistant activities *gradually* erode authority, working quietly to undermine an opponent who would probably win any open confrontation:

> The goal, after all . . . is not directly to overthrow or transform a system of domination but rather to survive—today, this week, this season—within it. (Scott 1985: 301)

Resistance therefore serves to "impose limitations on a system of power which allow[s] those in authority to exercise unlimited control" (B. Morris 1988: 33–34). In the specific context of institutional confinement, resistance thus operates as a loose collection of daily activities undertaken by inmates for "working the system to their minimum disadvantage" (Hobsbawm 1973: 7).

In stark contrast to accounts of dramatic riots and rebellions that fill criminological studies of institutional confinement, Scott's ethnography reveals small gaps in the exercise of dominance. His study of rural Southeast Asian communities examines the times, places, and conditions that provide subordinates with the ability to shift between moments of visible and opaque existence. Such transient moments, Scott suggests, can be appropriated for the mobilization of resistance. Applying Scott's model to an ethnographic study of power relations in the Aboriginal town of Doomadgee in northern Australia, David Trigger (1992) spatially maps co-existing domains of "Blackfella" authority in the residential zone of the fringe settlement and juxtaposes them with the "Whitefella" zones of administrative, medical, and religious authority. Confined within the institutional structures of a colonial system that dispossessed the region's Aboriginal peoples in the late nineteenth century, the indigenous "inmates" of Doomadgee respond resistantly by maintaining socially closed (opaque) Blackfella domains and transgressing Whitefella hegemony by preserving certain traditional forms of politics and law. As chapter 4 demonstrates, studies of resistance in sites of institutional confinement reveal opaque spaces and moments in the camp, school, hospital, or prison where inmates subvert institutional surveillance long enough to acknowledge, coordinate, and maintain their own alternative and informal organizations (Casella 2001; Starr 2001; Prentice and Prentice 2000; Burton et al. 1999; Lindauer 1996; Dennis 1995).

As the Scott and Trigger case studies indicate, to be truly resistant, obstructive activities must surpass individual experience. Both tacit and openly acknowledged coordination must occur within the subordinate group for participants to create and defend their secluded spaces. From the cooperation that results in patterns of concealed and shared insubordination, Scott derives the term "hidden transcripts" to refer to the nonelite, undocumented, and anonymous everyday events that accumulate as a powerful expression of collective resistance:

> Under the appropriate conditions, the accumulation of petty acts can, rather like snowflakes on a steep mountainside, set off an avalanche. (Scott 1990: 192)

Interrogating Diversity: Reform, Respite, Ritual

For collective actions to be coordinated and undertaken, however, resistance must be consolidated, organized, and focused (Miller and Tilley 1984). As Scott explains, some equal and oppositional form of sanctioning power is required to ensure that

> Any subordinate who seeks privilege by ingratiating himself to his superior will have to answer for that conduct once he returns to the world of his peers. In situations of systematic subordination such sanctions may go well beyond scolding and insult to physical coercion, as in the beating

of an informer by prisoners. Social pressure among peers . . . is by itself a powerful weapon of subordinates. (1990: 191)

Thus, to be properly considered a counter-hegemony, a hidden transcript must itself be "uniform, cohesive and bound by powerful mutual sanctions that hold competing discourses at arm's length" (Scott 1990: 135). Out of this perpetual struggle between two competing worlds—that of the owners, masters, and staff and that of the workers, servants, and inmates—the dual and oppositional roles of "us" versus "them" emerge and are maintained.

Both feminist and postcolonial scholarship in archaeology have critiqued the basic assumptions framing this traditional paradigm of domination and resistance. Many regard its dualistic structure as a limited product of modernist, essentialist, masculinist, or Eurocentric thought (Julian Thomas 2002; Trocolli 1999; Kent 1999; Johnson 1999; Nelson 1997; Spencer-Wood 1996, 1999). Others express dissatisfaction with its inherent emphasis on dynamics of aggression, struggle, and conflict, arguing that "us"/"them" approaches produce simplistic, reactive, and somewhat static interpretations of power that in turn mask crucial historical, social, and personal aspects of diversity (Tarlow 2002; Gero 2000; Meskell 1996; De Cunzo 1995).

In her poststructuralist attempt to transcend binary modes of analysis in literary studies, Judith Butler questions the wider modes of power that legitimate specific categories for people in Western society (Butler 1993; 1997). Her basic aim is not to abolish foundational categories, but rather to interrogate what aspects of identity become authorized and, conversely, what aspects are excluded or foreclosed. Applied to an institutional context, Butler's approach prompts consideration of how the multiple, situational, conflicting, and opportunistic experiences of power within staff and inmate groups become masked or consolidated—through peer pressure and institutional structures—into rigid "us" versus "them" categories (Liebling and Price 2001; Tonry and Petersilia 2000; Conover 2000; Rideau 1995; Jim Thomas 1993; Gelsthorpe and Morris 1990). As penal sociologist Adrian Howe observes (1994: 173), the shift in focus enabled by a multirelational approach has helped scholars reject institutional categories of analysis (such as guard, inmate, or patient) as essentialized or absolute identities within places of confinement. Instead, these familiar labels can be understood as open to continuous and productive contestation between different groups of institutional subjects.

Converging on poststructuralist routes, a number of scholars over the last twenty years have interrogated the embodied state of institutional confinement in order to emphasize a *diversity* of experiences endured by different kinds of institutional inhabitants. By characterizing patterns in the living conditions experienced by various types of staff, visitors, professional specialists, and inmates, scholars have exposed the multiple forms of subjectivity created in places of confinement. While historians and archaeologists undertaking this research have tended to chart the transformations of embodied institutional practices over the centuries (Baugher 2001; Piddock 2001; Christianson 1998; Gilchrist 1994; Rafter 1990; Freedman 1981; Irwin 1980), sociologists, anthropologists, criminologists, social activists, and health reformers have tended to expose patterns of poverty, illness, disability, gender inequality, and racism that shape current experiences of institutional confinement (Snyder and Mitchell 2001; Carlen 1998; Owen 1998; Haney 1997; Bowler 1997; Carroll 1997; Naffine 1996; Prendergast et al. 1995; Irwin and Austin 1994; Fleisher 1989; Lombardo 1989; Prout and Ross 1988; Irwin 1985; Bowker 1981).

Archaeologist Lu Ann De Cunzo suggests that institutional life can be interpreted as an interplay among three separate material dynamics: a paternalistic imposition of reform; a negotiated period of respite; and an embodied experience of ritual. By contrasting these dynamics throughout her detailed study of the Magdalen Society of Philadelphia—an urban-based asylum for "fallen" women that operated from 1800 to 1915—De Cunzo represents both the history and archaeology of the institution as a complicated and subtly nuanced "conversation" between competing aims, objectives, and intentions held by different groups of inhabitants (2001). As a venue for moral improvement, the asylum was established by city elites and run by middle-class staff to reform wayward souls through labor. The internal material world—uniforms, repetitive work assignments, meal etiquette, ceramic tablewares, kitchen, bedchambers, front parlor—were designed to cultivate within inmates a purified feminine identity.

Of course, such lofty aims inevitably clashed with the interests of young, unmarried, sexually active, working-class female inmates, who "settled on a strategy to survive their incarceration and use the institution for their own ends" (De Cunzo 1995: 113). Rejecting institutional definitions of guilt and wretchedness, the Magdalens themselves did not internalize any disciplinary process of improvement, atonement, or moral redemption. Rather, documentary evidence suggests they relied upon the facility as "a refuge and a respite from disease, the prison or almshouse, unhappy family situations, abusive men, and dire economic circumstances" (De Cunzo 1995: 132).

To the interplay of reform and respite in her multirelational model, De Cunzo adds a third dynamic—one that offers a further theoretical direction for studies of incarceration and confinement. Drawing from anthropological studies of ritualized activities (Bell 1992; Turner 1969; Douglas 1966), De Cunzo interprets the daily regimen, architectural layout, and material assemblages of the asylum site as embodied modes of symbolic transformation. Linking patterns of individual experience to the "continual process of constituting society and comprehending the cosmos," the daily rituals that structured the Magdalen Society serve to emphasize the role of the physical body as both a metaphor and map of social power (De Cunzo 1995: 114; 2006). Thus, as detailed in chapter 4, De Cunzo's multirelational approach illuminates a diversity of experiences—linked to a wide range of institutional occupants—through archaeological interpretation of the multisensory and embodied ritual practices of individuals in the asylum.

Scholarship emphasizing diversity in places of confinement has focused not only on different kinds of individual inmate experiences, but also on differences in the type and nature of the institutional systems themselves. As penologist David Garland has observed, even generic images of late twentieth-century institutions offer only a partial perspective on the wider social functions of contemporary confinement:

> To represent the business of punishment in quasi-scientific terms, and to organize penal practices accordingly, promotes a particular image of the state and of its authority, and of its relationship to offenders and other citizens. Indeed, it has been argued . . . that the official adoption of scientific languages and rehabilitative forms in modern penal institutions has sometimes had more to do with the cultural symbolism involved than with the desire fully to implement the practices they imply. (Garland 1990: 257)

Thus, in addition to foregrounding diversity in the experiences of various institutional inhabitants, scholars have begun to consider underlying historical, socioeconomic, gendered, and administrative differences in the institutional systems themselves.

The confinement of women has particularly challenged normative models of institutional systems, as tensions between domestic and disciplinary ideologies of social control have struggled for primacy since the Civil War era (Freedman 1981: 90). A number of historians and sociologists have even suggested that enough difference had emerged between male and female institutional systems by 1870 to warrant the idea of distinct "feminised penal practices" (Rafter 1985: 288–90; see also Howe 1994; Gelsthorpe and Morris 1990; Carlen 1983).

Adopting a firm socioeconomic position, Nicole Rafter (1985) links the proliferation of disciplinary modes of institutionalization to wider dynamics of class, gender, and race disenfranchisement over the late nineteenth century. Questioning the "sisterliness" Estelle Freedman poses as the central relationship between reformers and prisoners (1981), Rafter demonstrates a hardening of divisions between social classes and racial groups during the industrial era. Growing antipathies eventually erupted in an almost stereotypical clash between inmate and reformer in late Victorian institutions for women:

> Two groups of women—the working-class offenders and the middle-class reformers—met, so to speak, at the gate of the women's reformatory. The struggle between them was economically functional in some ways to the reformers: it helped maintain a pool of cheap domestic labour for women like themselves, and, by keeping women in the surplus labour force, it undergirded the economic system to which they owed their privileged position. (Rafter 1985: 175)

Archaeologists and architectural historians have similarly emphasized a temporal shift in institutional temperaments and regimes. Outlined in chapter 2, their work has disclosed a profound material transition from the more domestic and benevolent eighteenth-century asylums to the brutal utilitarian regimes of early nineteenth-century institutions (Baugher 2001; Spencer-Wood and Baugher 2001; Lucas 1999; Markus 1993).

In sum, a richer understanding of the modern institution requires an appreciation of variation in terms of both the historically contingent forms and socially constructed experiences of confinement. Arguing for just this kind of "holistic" perspective, De Cunzo (2006) foregrounds the material dynamic of "ritual practice" as a route for linking particular types of institutions back to the diverse embodied experiences of inhabitants. Observing that institutions exist not only to detain, but also to teach, heal, accommodate, and inspire occupants toward religious devotion or personal transformation, De Cunzo argues that studies of ritual spaces in institutions will help scholars consider how different individuals endured different types of disciplinary control and how those experiences in turn linked inhabitants back to the society beyond the perimeter walls.

Expanding Goffman's model of institutionalization with an archaeological metaphor, De Cunzo theorizes institutional practices as a *sedimentary* process—a gradual concretion of regulated events, everyday activities, and material experiences that ultimately fabricate the institutional consciousness of the individual inmate. By focusing her research on individuals' experiential, personal, and bodily encounters with the institution, De Cunzo embraces issues of diversity and thus avoids Foucault's seductive reduction of *all* institutional experience to the manufacture of uniform "docile bodies" (1977). Reading institutional identities as the sedimentation of ritualized practices, De Cunzo introduces an alternative theoretical model for understanding the multiple lived experiences of institutional confinement.

Strategies of Negotiation: On Coping, Survival, and Exchange

But do sedimented or ritualized practices themselves constitute a mode of discipline? Regardless of how guards, inmates, patients, visitors, or administrators individually experience their own embodied activity, the daily institutional ritual—or "repetitive . . . formal, stylized, and symbolic action"—ultimately serves to "*transform* and *remake* the individual" by "persuading the body first" through orchestrated performances (De Cunzo 1995: 114, original emphasis). Perhaps individuals internalize institutional discipline through the very ritualization of those diverse embodied actions and encounters. More to the point, can scholars adequately illuminate such highly individualized and embodied experiences of confinement?

Research by both ethnographers and penologists continues to struggle with the profound inaccessibility and opacity of institutional life (Rhodes 2001; Hornblum 1998; Feldman 1991). Particularly in the case of prisons, inmates may have far too little privacy to comfortably tolerate the intrusion of a researcher into their social world (Owen 1998). Within these stark institutional environments, knowledge itself operates as a mode of power—a feature not lost on Foucault in his explorations of the modern carceral society (1977, 1980). By seeking to gather knowledge about those who experience incarceration, do fieldworkers themselves participate in a form of scholarly surveillance? Particularly during ethnographic studies, the researcher's paradoxical entanglement both with those who incarcerate and those who are incarcerated can force a more acute awareness of the cryptic experiences of restraint, discipline, mortification, insubordination, and complicity that shape institutional environments. But despite this worthy adoption of self-reflexivity, the researcher's implicit attempt to reveal individual bodily experiences of confinement may serve to reinforce, if not extend, the scope of institutional discipline.

Ultimately, concern over issues of diversity and plurality, embodied experience, institutional opacity, and accidental collusion have fermented dissatisfaction with simple definitions of power as a binary hierarchy of domination and resistance, with both forces locked in perpetual antagonism. Instead, as observed earlier in this chapter, scholars have begun to consider alternative forms of power relations, applying concepts of "heteroglossia" (Bakhtin 1981), "interacting modes of power" (Wolf 1990), "social distinctions" (Moore 1994), and "powers with" (Spencer-Wood 1999) to theorize the fluid interplay of negotiations, adaptations, and improvisations in the performance of power relations.

Returning to the idea of heterarchy, an increasing number of archaeologists have conceptualized power as a set of social relations characterized by their numerous, varying, and circumstantial connections (Ehrenreich et al. 1995; Crumley 1987). In this theoretical model, power operates as moments of opportunity rather than as binary conflicts or bodily experiences. By emphasizing the lateral, nested, and plural nature of power relations, scholars who utilize the concept of heterarchy have interrogated the "several cross-cutting personal criteria [which] contribute to status, influence, and power" (J. E. Levy 1999: 73). When applied to carceral settings, a heterarchical perspective supports exploration of the situational means by which institutional inhabitants mobilize transient moments of power to negotiate their austere environment.

Surviving Confinement

Coping in an institution is itself an expression of lateral and circumstantial power. Out of sociologists' and criminologists' examination of the distress created by confinement (Mathiesen 1990; Fleisher 1989; Toch 1977; Cohen 1954), a distinct group of now-classic studies of institutional subcultures emerged between the late 1940s and 1970s. Characterizing incarceration as a series of "pains," Gresham Sykes (1958) argued that institutional life imposes a series of deprivations upon inmates: deprivation of liberty and freedom of movement; deprivation of goods and services; deprivation of gendered and sexual identity; deprivation of autonomy; and deprivation of personal security. Other studies detail the carceral influences that force inmates to undergo "prisonization" (Clemmer 1940) or assimilation into the "code of inmate solidarity" (Garofalo and Clark 1985; Sykes and Messinger 1960).

How do patients, inmates, and prisoners cope with extreme conditions of material deprivation and personal anxiety? Drawing from psychological models of adaptation, scholars have identified constructive regimes that provide activity, opportunities for change, social contact, and material support—inmate responses, in other words, that ameliorate the worst pains of confinement. Defined as "coping," this constellation of behaviors is adopted to help keep anguish and distress under control (Gallo and Ruggiero 1991). While recognized as always "partial, unstable and arduous" (Liebling 2000: 288), such coping activities enable inmates to personally adjust to the process of institutionalization.

In his classic sociology of asylum life, Erving Goffman found that institutional conditions typically produce four types of inmate response (1961: 61–63). Among the inmates he observed, most experienced at least an initial period of "situational withdrawal," during which they retreated from everything except events immediately surrounding their bodies. Also termed "regression" in psychiatric literature and "acute depersonalization" in criminological studies, this reaction can extend to become a more general response to institutional life.

Alternatively, some inmates responded to institutional discipline with "intransigent" tactics—intentionally challenging the surrounding institutional system by flagrantly refusing to cooperate with staff members. However, because sustained rejection requires an intimate familiarity with the formal organization of an institution, such a coping strategy paradoxically breeds a "deep kind of involvement in the establishment" (Goffman 1961: 62).

The third and fourth inmate responses Goffman identified involve varying degrees of compliance or internalization of the disciplinary system. When an inmate experiences "colonization," he or she accepts living conditions in the total institution and achieves a relatively contented existence through acquisition of institutional privileges. Such inmates can be characterized as "having found a home" in their place of confinement. In contrast, some inmates experience "conversion" or the active adoption of the official view of themselves and other inmates. Such inmates—Foucault's "docile bodies" (1977)—respond to institutional confinement by attempting to act out the role of the *perfect* inmate. In some cases inmates even adopt characteristics of the staff, including styles of dress or language, to express their internal reform.

Studies of female institutions suggest that during confinement women adopt coping strategies different from those of men (Owen 1998; Naffine 1996). Although researchers have documented distinctive inmate subcultures and conduct codes in female institutions (Jensen and Jones 1976; Heffernan 1972), women appear to be less committed to these particular coping mechanisms than their male counterparts (Ward and Kassebaum 1965). A somewhat lurid fascination with "fictive kinship structures" (Giallombardo 1966: 159) has particularly flourished in research literature on women's confinement, with scholars linking the social and emotional support roles of "mommy," "daddy," "daughter," "sibling," "husband," or "wife" within a "play family" to such inmate attributes as age, physical appearance, sexual identity, ethnic or socioeconomic background, and institutional experience (T. W. Foster 1975; Heffernan 1972). Women's adherence to such inmate codes appears to relate to the length of institutional sentence (Tittle and Tittle 1964), type of institutional facility (Wilson 1986), strength of external familial bonds (Jones 1993; Zingraff and Zingraff 1980), and the influence of staff expectations (Kruttschnitt 1981).

Within male institutions, racial dynamics have complicated classic models of inmate coping strategies. Reflecting on his earlier research, sociologist John Irwin observes:

> There is no longer a single, overarching convict culture or social organization, as there tended to be twenty years ago. . . . Most prisoners restrict their associations to a few other prisoners and withdraw from prison public life. A minority associates with gangs, gamble, buy and sell contra-

band commodities, and engage in prison homosexual behavior. If they do so, however, they must act "tough" and be willing to live by the new code, that is, be ready to meet threats of violence with violence. (1990 [1970]: vi)

Particularly since the 1970s, with the advent of mass incarceration of African-Americans and Latinos in America, inmate solidarity has reassembled along racial affiliations (Parenti 1999). The "convict code" has been effectively replaced by a more violent "code of the street":

"Supergangs," such as the Disciplines, El Rukn, Vice Lords, and Latin Kings in Illinois, the Mexican Mafia, Black Guerrilla Family, and Aryan Brotherhood in California, and the Netas in New York City, have taken over the illicit economy of the prison and destabilized the entire social system of inmates, forcing the latter to shift from "doing your own time" to "doing gang time." (Wacquant 2001: 97)

As a testimony to their subversive power, these racial gangs have even forced a comprehensive administrative restructuring of state correctional systems in Illinois, California, and Texas (Martin and Ekland-Olson 1987; Fox 1982). As the same urban street gangs thrive on both sides of the institutional perimeter wall, the adoption of this particular coping strategy further obscures the distinction between freedom and confinement for ethnic communities in American society (Parenti 1999).

Reciprocity: The Dynamics of "Making Do"

Since the dangers of bullying, self-harming, and suicide all too frequently accompany attempts to "go it alone" in institutions, most inmates accept that everyday survival (or "making do") requires some form of sociality—some mode of social, emotional, and material support. In other words, to cope with institutional confinement, one must trade.

As first argued by the French anthropologist Marcel Mauss, there are no free gifts (1990 [1950]). In all non-monetary economies, the exchange of objects generates legal, moral, social, and sexual obligations. Trade, or the giving of gifts, consists of three crucial obligations: to give, to receive, and to reciprocate (or counter-gift). Exchange thus forms a cycle of obligations, as counter-gifts themselves become gifts. Through reciprocity, participants become knitted together in a social and temporal web of relationships. Failure to engage any one of these obligations "is tantamount to declaring war; it is to reject the bond of alliance and commonality" (Mauss 1990 [1950]: 13). Thus, trade cycles bind people into wider networks of connections, into circumstantial and heterarchical power relations materially enacted through the flow of gifts.

Within an institutional environment, participation in the trade cycle is not limited to those confined. Some degree of staff collusion inevitably occurs and is necessary to maintain routes of access into and around the institutional compound. Additionally, it is not merely objects that enter into exchange. Indeed, the term "libido" has been adopted by some scholars to describe the yearnings or cravings that fuel social trade (Bourdieu 1998: 76–79). Information, knowledge, "kites" (illicit messages), and even sexual encounters can all serve as potentially valuable commodities (Clemmer 1940). However, as the material elements of exchange provide physical evidence of its existence, possession of contraband earns the greatest official sanctions.

Given that such sanctions can include months of solitary confinement for the guilty inmate or dishonorable expulsion for the staff member, why would inhabitants engage in such risky and subversive coping strategies? Participation in what is variously called a black market or "sub rosa" economic system (V. L. Williams and Fish 1974) fulfils four generalized types of yearning or desire. Typically, the institutional black market satisfies various physiological cravings for food, personal safety, or sexual activity inadequately provided through official routes. Underground trade also supports a range of addictions, supplying contraband cigarettes, alcohol, and drugs for the right price. Trade networks and relations of obligation also create a form of reciprocal solidarity among inmate subgroups and between inmates and complicit members of the institutional staff.

Finally, drawing from later anthropological and sociological reinterpretations of gift exchange (Godelier 1999; Bourdieu 1998; Lévi-Strauss 1987), mobilizations of power, influence, and social status can be seen to effectively fuel trade. People give, according to these studies, in order to achieve that powerful position of being "owed" a counter-gift. They are giving in the anticipation of receiving. However, and most crucial, the reciprocal act of fulfillment (or counter-gifting) must be delayed. Exchange is thereby organized to maximize the number of debts and obligations that can be simultaneously created and maintained (Gregory 1982).

It is this obscure web of obligations—of favors, debts, yearnings, loans, and extortions—that structures the daily experience of institutional confinement (V. L. Williams and Fish 1974). Ultimately, exchange cycles infuse all forms of making do. Further, trade encompasses not only material, but social, gendered, and sexual forms of reciprocity (Weiner 1992; Strathern 1988). Mauss himself recognizes this delicate fusion of the objectified and the embodied, observing that "to make a gift of something to someone is to make a present of some part of oneself" (Mauss 1990 [1950]: 12).

From an archaeological perspective, transactional coping strategies hold profound material implications. Not only can the smuggling of contraband into and around places of confinement produce distinctive artifact patterns in the archaeological record of institutional sites (Casella 2002; Bush 2000; Wurtzburg and Hahn 1992b; Cotter et al. 1988), but contextual analysis of these hidden transcripts can also demonstrate a wide range of emotive, familial, conjugal, and ethnic bonds maintained by those who endure confinement (Casella 2000; Burton et al. 1999; Lindauer 1996). Material signatures of such trade include modifications to original institutional designs, including the reinforcement or augmentation of perimeter walls, stockades, and internal fencing or the addition of surveillance towers and guard stations. Similarly, artifactual assemblages can also reveal the internal nature of illicit exchange, with extra rations, diverting luxuries, tokens of value, or discard stashes appearing in the material record.

The recent proliferation of "super-maximum" penitentiaries across America—most infamously including Pelican Bay State Prison in California and Marion Federal Prison in Illinois—can be read as a tacit response to the critical significance of sociality, encounter, and exchange in prisoner coping strategies. Designed to enforce the "hyperisolation" of especially violent, dangerous, and recalcitrant felons, these places of extreme confinement impose a profound and chronic alienation upon those incarcerated (Haney 1997). Deprived of all meaningful activity, inmates are isolated not only from each other, but from all sensory experience of the natural world. Minimal accommodation is provided in single-person pods of concrete and reinforced plastic. Through both the austere institutional layout and video monitoring systems, a comprehensive surveillance of all guard and inmate activities is perpetually maintained. Because such vigorous regimes of containment and isolation breed mental disorders and exacerbate preexisting medical conditions (Lovell et al. 2000; Kupers 1999), these high-tech "total institutions" further blur the distinction between asylums, hospitals, and prisons. In merging institutional types, do super-max prisons represent the apotheosis of carceral society in America? Or a return to premodern methods of warehousing those who threaten society? Would Jeremy Bentham feel pride or confusion as a witness to his institutional legacy?

Conclusion

This chapter has considered various explanations of why and how institutions operate. Classic philosophical and criminological arguments emphasize the shifting roles of punishment, reform, and deterrence as rationales for confinement. In contrast, Michel Foucault's compelling model of penality questions the exertion and rejection of discipline within the modern institution. Frustrated by the reduction of institutional life to a binary opposition of domination and resistance, other scholars propose a relocation of power into the individual and collective inmate body. By charting multiple embodied experiences of confinement, the significant diversity of both those who inhabit institutions and the historically situated institutional systems themselves can be illuminated. Finally, an interest in the methods by which institutional inhabitants negotiate their confinement has led a number of researchers to consider the various material coping strategies adopted by inmates and staff. Initiated by inhabitants seeking to ameliorate the worst deprivations and pains of confinement, networks of favor and obligation knit institutional occupants into circumstantial and transient relationships of power.

By way of conclusion, we must again consider the critical question "why confine?" Does institutional confinement ultimately operate as a means of sustaining social order? Of managing the shifts of a fluid labor market? Of punishing individuals for their selfish, violent, or repugnant actions? Or of neutralizing those dangerous anomalies and aberrant forms which threaten the very fabric of society? Institutional confinement does provide a powerful technology for purging undesirables—even if, in the case of high-tech, supermax facilities, this same technology begins to converge with forms of torture as defined by international human rights covenants (BBC 2006). All theoretical paths explored by these questions converge at the relationship between the state and its citizenry. All investigate the process by which institutional confinement simultaneously reconstructs the citizen self and identifies the anomalous other—the unproductive other, the criminal other, and the racial, ethnic or cultural other.

What is the function of institutional confinement as we move into the twenty-first century? In his critical assessment of incarceration in modern state societies, John Pratt (2002) links the progressive liberal agenda of "community sentencing," "work-release schemes," and "corrective treatment programs" to a strategic sanitization of institutional confinement. As politicians currently struggle with the fiscal realities of mass incarceration, the carceral regime supports greater inmate contact and integration with outside society. For Pratt, institutions serve as custodial places of supervised liberty rather than as punitive detention facilities.

Alternatively, Thomas Mathiesen (1990) distinguishes five summary and overlapping ideological functions served by institutional confinement. Institutions first serve a deterrent or "action function" by providing the most publicly observable type of sanction available to the modern state. However, by locating aberrations and dangers safely behind perimeter walls, the institution serves a secondary "diverting function," by channeling society's attention away from "the dangers flowing from those in power" (Mathiesen 1990: 138). Purging unproductive noncontributors from wider capitalist society, confinement serves a "power-draining function." It incapacitates society's dangerous rogue elements (or those with too much time to fill) by safely warehousing them inside institutions.

Confinement, of course, also serves a crucial "symbolic function," since those caught in the institution are stigmatized as a "*monstruum*—a being whose features are inherently different from ours" (Melossi 2000: 311). Increasingly, this stigmatized inmate is imagined as a dark monster, as "young African-American men from the inner city have come to personify the explosive mix of moral degeneracy and mayhem" (Wacquant 2001: 104). With mounting expenditures and political efforts subsumed in the drive to separate these "monsters" from mainstream society, the symbolic and diversionary functions of institutional confinement converge. Finally, as warehouses for exiles, institutions serve a basic "expurgatory function." Large populations of violent and unproductive others are removed from society, accommodated, controlled, and conveniently forgotten. In purging these undesirables from the body politic, the state effectively quarantines dangerous and polluting influences away from the citizenry.

In the next chapter, we will explore how American institutional confinement has materially evolved, from its early colonial origins in the seventeenth century through its increasingly ubiquitous presence over the course of the twentieth. Archaeologists have adopted myriad philosophical approaches to interpret the built fabric, portable artifacts, and stratigraphic residues of these historic American institutions. Case studies can be grouped by three general types of institutional sites: places of punishment, places of asylum, and places of exile. Through a detailed exploration of historic sites related to these categories, chapter 4 will consider the enduring material legacy of this uniquely modern social phenomenon.

An Archaeology of Institutional Confinement

Drawing upon the historical and theoretical themes previously discussed, this chapter will examine archaeological perspectives on the American experience of institutional confinement. Adopting both functionalist and experiential approaches, the following case studies demonstrate how social power tangibly operates in the modern institution and how such material experiences themselves generate a distinctive worldview for those who inhabit places of confinement.

Over the past three decades, much work has been undertaken on a wide range of institutional sites across America. While important philosophical themes of punishment, involuntary labor, citizenship and civil rights, personal dignity, social identity, discipline, and inmate resistance can be traced throughout these case studies, places of confinement can also be usefully grouped according to three categories: punishment, asylum, and exile. By distinguishing institutions according to the intended *purpose* of confinement, these three analytic categories reveal distinct populations of noncitizens in the modern capitalist state: those who are criminal; those who are dependent; and those who are politically or racially disenfranchised. This chapter provides archaeological perspectives on their material experiences under institutional confinement.

Confinement as Punishment

Serving as the most iconic and sublime form of institutional confinement, penal incarceration has changed profoundly over the last two centuries. Archaeological research on prisons has explored the material implications of the broad philosophical patterns informing these changes, as evolving concepts of punishment, moral reform, and citizenship shaped the American institutional landscape. Through examination of associated material culture and architectural landscapes, archaeologists have illuminated daily life experiences, labor regimes, coping mechanism, exertions of repression and insubordination, and expressions of personal agency and identity forged in American penal establishments.

The Walnut Street Prison (Pennsylvania)

Designed in 1774 by the architect Robert Smith, the Walnut Street Prison achieved historical notoriety as America's first experiment in modern institutional design. Representing the first manifestation of a "centralized state apparatus" in the New World (Takagi 1993: 542), the prison explicitly adopted new disciplinary technologies to transform the individual criminal into a rehabilitated citizen (Foucault 1977). Constructed of stone, the primary facade of the two-story neoclassical building extended 184 feet (56 m.) along Walnut Street, directly across from the Pennsylvania State House yard (later renamed Independence Square) in central Philadelphia (Cotter et al. 1988: 17; see also figure 2.3). Flanked by two symmetrical wings of 90 feet (27.5 m.), the U-shaped compound was surrounded by a perimeter wall 20 feet (6 m.) high. To improve fireproofing and security, the ceramic tiled floors of this first purpose-designed American prison were supported with stone groin vaults. While some prisoners were transferred in by early 1776, over the subsequent years of the Revolutionary War, the building was commandeered by the American Army for use as a military hospital.

By the early 1790s, the prison had been repaired and restored to its original civilian functions. In concert with emerging eighteenth-century penal philosophies, the Walnut Street Prison cultivated inmate reform through constant industry, religious contemplation, and supervision. Administered through a strictly regimented daily schedule, the prison provided an early hybrid of Enlightenment rationale infused with American republican ideals. As a result, the Walnut Street Prison has been characterized as a direct ancestor of *both* the Auburn and Pennsylvania systems of punishment—the competing carceral templates that dominated penal reform debates during the subsequent Jacksonian era of the early nineteenth century (Garman 2005; Takagi 1993; Friedman 1993).

From 1795, prison workshops were added to the original penal compound, with facilities for iron nail manufacture, stone cutting and polishing, and carpentry arranged around a central exercise yard (Cotter et al. 1988: 21). Despite the initial rehabilitative goals, living conditions in the new prison rapidly declined because of overcrowding. By 1822, the facility incarcerated approximately 804 male and female prisoners in sex-segregated dormitory wards. With the rise of passionate reformist debates over penal isolation and surveillance during the Jacksonian era, the Walnut Street Prison was deemed functionally obsolete. Replaced by the Eastern State Penitentiary at Cherry Hill (1829), Moyamensing Debtor's Jail (1834), and Western State Penitentiary of Pittsburgh (1826), the Walnut Street Prison was demolished in 1835—ending its remarkable forty-year history as the first American institution dedicated to modern penal confinement.

During the spring of 1973, archaeological research sampled the southeastern corner of the original penal compound. Uncovering subsurface remains of the prison workshops, excavation trenches examined the final surviving component of the original prison grounds. Laid out in a grid of 5-foot (1.5 m.) squares, a total of twenty-six test pits were opened (Cotter et al. 1988: 26). Revealing two prison workshops, the project investigated the architectural relationship between penal confinement and unfree labor in this early American institution. The presence of fine sand and polished Pennsylvania marble fragments in stratigraphic deposits suggested that trenches had located the stonecutting and adjoining nail manufacture facilities recorded in late eighteenth-century historic plans. Subsurface foundations consisted of approximately 25 inches (63.5 cm.) of undressed schist stone footings, overlaid with walls of hand-molded bricks manufactured from local clays (Cotter et al. 1988: 29). The interior wall, dividing between the excavated workshops, was approximately 13 inches (33 cm.) thick, laid in courses of English bond. Serving as part of the institutional perimeter boundary, the larger exterior wall of the prison workshops was roughly 18 inches (46 cm.) thick, its English bond masonry containing an extra course of brick stretchers. Extended to a total depth of 104 inches (2.64 m.) from the modern surface, this massive wall feature demonstrated the careful fabrication of security that guided the design of this early American prison.

A total of 242 bags of artifacts were recovered from excavation trenches, with most of these objects collected from either the layers of demolition debris or the mixed fill contained within original wall footing features. Ceramics included transfer-printed and shell-edged pearlwares, tin-glazed delftwares, plain lead-glazed and slipped redwares, and cobalt blue–painted salt-glazed stonewares. Sherds of both hand-painted Chinese export porcelain and rim-molded creamwares were recovered in notable concentrations from the lower levels of fill. Although these relatively higher-value artifacts were interpreted as intrusions from the debtor's prison to the south of the workshop complex (Cotter et al. 1988: 48), more recent studies of American almshouses have linked similarly anomalous objects to wider fashionable practices of philanthropic charity among the more fortunate classes.

Researchers also examined the nature of prison labor in this early institution. Excavations suggested the presence of button manufacturing, with fifteen shell blanks, forty-four bone blanks, and nine bone buttons recovered. Since other sewing-related artifacts were recovered from an exterior midden deposit immediately adjacent to the southern workshop (Cotter et al. 1988: 71), prisoners were probably engaged in tailoring or uniform production in addition to the historically documented industries of nail manufacture, carpentry, and stonecutting.

Inmates also appeared to have co-opted institutional resources for more clandestine forms of production. Excavations recovered fourteen small fragments of worked bone in both cubic and rectangular shapes. Since two of the cubes had been marked with dots, the assemblage suggested a covert manufacture of bone dice occurred within prison workshops. Providing a mechanism for both personal amusement and prohibited gaming activities among inmates, these illicit objects suggest that alternative exchange networks structured the socioeconomic world of this institution. (See chapter 3 for a more detailed discussion of inmate coping and exchange strategies.)

Finally, research on the Walnut Street Prison involved a detailed application of Stanley South's classic methodology for analysis of artifact patterns in American historical sites (1977). Assemblages were first divided into groups according to South's functional categories (such as kitchen, architectural, furniture, arms, clothing, et cetera). Relative concentrations of these functional groups were then calculated by both number count and percentage. When this table of ratios was compared against the characteristic "artifact patterns" of South's ideal model sites, a close correlation emerged between artifact ratios from the Walnut Street Prison collection and those of a domestic site characterized by South as the "Carolina Artifact Pattern" site (Cotter et al. 1988: 58–62). On one hand, this comparative analysis suggests that—at least before imposition of austere institutional systems in the Jacksonian era—life under institutional confinement during the early nineteenth century retained an essentially domestic quality.

Conversely, since the Carolina Artifact Pattern was generated from archaeological investigations of a Southern plantation site—its antebellum socioeconomics reliant upon enslaved African-Americans—the archaeological correlation might equally demonstrate a shared materiality between different systems of unfree labor. Ultimately, these results suggest that before the Civil War, the everyday experience of noninstitutional agrarian enslavement may not have been materially dissimilar from that of penal incarceration. More recently, scholarly research on American penal institutions has turned to explicitly consider the archaeological implications of these material patterns, examining the role of unfree labor as a structuring regime under institutional confinement.

Old Rhode Island Penitentiary (Rhode Island)

Constructed in 1835 as one of the grand new reformist institutions of the Jacksonian era, the Old Rhode Island Penitentiary occupied Great Point, a low-lying cove to the east of Providence. Initial architectural plans were guided by an ideological passion for criminal rehabilitation. With the employment of John Haviland, the architect previously responsible for design of the Eastern State Penitentiary of Pennsylvania, Rhode Island state officials joined the fractious national debate over progressive penal reform by adopting the Separate system for inmate reform.

Nonetheless, when faced with costs associated with the construction and operation of a facility devoted to the strict isolation of inmates, civic leaders rapidly modified Haviland's designs to reduce both the size and scope of the new institution (Garman 1999: 87–93). When the first transfers occurred in 1838, solitary accommodation was available for only forty felons. Over the subsequent five decades, a general process of "haphazard development" (Garman 2005: 65) came to characterize the architectural evolution of this penitentiary.

Emphasizing socioeconomic aspects of penal labor relations, James Garman's study offers an archaeological application of the Rusche and Kirchheimer hypothesis (1968), an influential philosophy of institutional deterrence discussed in chapter 3. Expanding their classic Marxist approach, Garman links the polyvalence of inmate production to a fluid combination of "[the] attitude of the individual worker, the degree of difficulty of a particular task, and the threats or incentives embedded in the completion of the task" (2005: 119). As a result of these complex variables, prison authorities grappled continuously with the nature, organization, and regulation of inmate labor in the Old Rhode Island Penitentiary. These tensions were reflected throughout the materiality of the historic institution. Originally operating under the Pennsylvania (or separate) plan, inmates were assigned to the solitary production of shoes in their individual cells—taskwork meant to achieve the twin goals of rehabilitative industry and strict isolation.

However, by the early 1840s, as costs associated with the Pennsylvania plan spiraled, state officials adopted the rival Auburn plan. Based on the principle of silent congregate labor rather than isolated individual labor, this new regime transformed the basic organization of the Old Rhode Island Penitentiary. In 1843, leather shoe production was replaced by the manufacture of decorative paper fans—a fashionable commodity particular suited to the large-scale assembly-line mode of production (Garman 2005: 133). The six different activities involved in making decorative fans required a diverse range of craft skills and technical competence, ranging from lacquering and stenciling to painting and wood turning. Inmates were assigned specific repetitive tasks along the assembly line, with production rates increased by the streamlining of individual skilled activities. More significantly, this labor scheme assisted the monitoring of individual worker progress; any deficiencies in either quality or pace were quickly identified and punished. Conversion to the Auburn plan became architecturally manifest between 1845 and 1850, with the gradual addition of communal workshops to the Old Rhode Island Penitentiary compound (Garman 1999: 106–10).

Despite these attempts at profit generation, labor under institutional confinement proved too rigidly structured to accommodate marketplace changes. By 1847, a nationwide consumer shift toward ribbed folding fans rendered decorative flat fans unfashionably obsolete. Faced with mounting financial losses, state officials ceased fan production in 1847 (Garman 2005: 140–41). Following election of a new prison governor that same year, a total reconfiguration of both the industrial and accommodational facilities was undertaken over the early 1850s. Rather than managing penal labor themselves, penal authorities sold the silent congregate labor of their charges to private contractors, earning a reliable return of forty cents per day for each male prisoner (Garman 2005: 145). Penitentiary accounts from 1877 document that both inmate labor and prison workshops were externally leased for the manufacture of shoes, cotton ties, and wire goods, as well as for carpentry and furniture construction.

Inmates challenged this system of unfree labor. Archaeological investigations have mapped collective patterns of resistance across the built environment of the Old Rhode Island Penitentiary, locating "intra-institutional" offenses from 1872 through 1877 by activity zone (Garman 2005: 170). Results suggest that recalcitrant behaviors predominated in the penitentiary workshops, with 60 percent of infractions, or 789 out of 1,306 documented events, occurring in this area. Representing more than 1.5 times the number recorded in all other areas combined, these inmate offenses represented challenges to the code of silence (talking, gazing around, or otherwise communicating), destruction of prison property (wasting stock, damaging work, or destroying tools), or general misconduct (disorderly conduct, refusing to work, stealing, neglectfulness, or fighting).

As noted in chapter 3, the experience of confinement is interpreted by some scholars as a heterarchy of power (J. E. Levy 1999) with transient groups of staff and inmates locked into a perpetual barter of circumstantial advantage within the institution (Wacquant 2001; Casella 2000; Fleisher 1989; V. L. Williams and Fish 1974; Heffernan 1972). In the case of the Old Rhode Island Penitentiary, researchers interpreted the efficacy of prisoner resistance through continuous modifications to the workshop structures, the built environment itself providing a durable record of staff responses to convict insubordination. A suspicious fire on January 14, 1874, deemed an act of malicious arson, eventually resulted in a harsh work schedule for reconstruction of the workshops by inmates. The new designs were explicitly celebrated as both impermeable and fireproof (Garman 2005: 175). Archaeological excavations on the eastern exterior of the 1854 workshop structure revealed cobble-lined pathways, each approximately 24 inches (61 cm.) wide. Connecting all points of access, this undocumented paving feature served as an architectural channel for inmate movement between places of labor (Garman 1999: 205). Finally, in a severe response to workplace resistance, authorities approved the construction of eight "dark cells" in the basement of the west wing. Used to punish repetitive or particularly heinous offenses, this cell block provided a technology of extreme confinement, subjecting residents to extended periods of complete sensory deprivation within a space of 4 by 6 feet (1.2 by 1.8 m.).

The built environment of institutional confinement offers fresh material perspectives on both the collective tensions that mobilized inmates toward resistance and the reciprocal architectural responses undertaken by institutional authorities. Close archival analysis can expose the basic disciplinary techniques and fiscal opportunism that structured prison industries. Other archaeological projects, such as the Old Baton Rouge Penitentiary we turn to next, illuminate the fluid boundaries between types of unfree labor as state-run penal institutions diffused beyond the New England region of the American Northeast.

Old Baton Rouge Penitentiary (Louisiana)

As the "carceral enthusiasm" of the Jacksonian era swept across the nation (Hirsch 1992: 66), institutional models of criminal management spread to the American South. By the early 1830s, Louisiana had erected its first state penitentiary in the central district of Baton Rouge. This establishment consisted of two monumental brick structures known as the upper and lower cell houses. Incarcerating a total of 440 inmates, each house contained four tiers of unventilated brick cells approximately 4 by 7 feet (1.2 by 2.1 m.) in dimension (B. Foster et al. 1995: 26). Two administrative quarters and a multipurpose hospital and workshop building completed the symmetrical U-shaped compound (Wurtzburg and Hahn 1992a). With Louisiana state officials, like their contemporaries in Rhode Island, adopting the more fiscally pragmatic Auburn plan from New York State, the Baton Rouge penitentiary was initially administered around a daily inmate routine of silent congregate labor. Early productive industries included cloth manufacture and tailoring; tanning and production of leather goods; carpentry, joinery, and cabinet making; gun and watch repair; and blacksmithing. By 1846, a dedicated cotton factory and engine house replaced the eastern brick perimeter wall, and the facility expanded to incarcerate a total inmate population of 622 men and 20 women.

With cheap industrial goods from the penitentiary workshops flooding the marketplace, local merchants began to lobby against the state's monopoly on unfree penal labor. In 1844, the Louisiana legislature forbade the sale of convict-manufactured commodities that competed against local private industries. As a direct result of this law, penitentiary systems of the American South rapidly diverged from the original template of the modern institution (Friedman 1993; McKelvey 1936). While lofty philosophical ideals of inmate reform may have troubled the philanthropic elites of Europe and the urbanized American Northeast, a far more pragmatic spirit guided the state officials of Louisiana. Instead of working within the confines of the prison, battalions of convicts were leased to private contractors for large-scale agriculture and construction work *outside* the penitentiary walls. In Louisiana, levee construction along the Mississippi River proved an ideal, if arduous and hazardous, works project for expendable convict labor (Carleton 1971: 11–13). Thus, by the final decades of the antebellum period, penal confinement in the American South emerged as a unique and distinctive system characterized by external, nonindustrial, and privatized forms of unfree labor. And with the dramatic increase in African-American inmates after the Civil War, the convict leasing system of the American South provided a terribly familiar alternative to the labor management system of African-American slavery that had previously structured the Southern economy (Parenti 1999; Christianson 1998; B. Foster 1995; Novak 1978; Carleton 1971).

As a demographic result of the convict leasing system, the Old Baton Rouge Penitentiary served primarily as a human warehouse. Over its eighty-four years of operation, the institution confined that small minority of Louisiana's inmate population that fell under one of three special categories: male convicts too sick or feeble to endure the inhumane conditions of private work camps; male convicts awaiting private lease assignment; and female convicts, who as a group were subjected to internal work detail rather than external contracted labor (Fisher-Giorlando 1995; Carleton 1971). By 1901, the population of incarcerated felons at the Baton Rouge penitentiary had dropped to a total of 128, with five listed as women (Nobles 2000: 7).

Archaeologically, the relative absence of institutional inmates produced a paucity of disposable goods and personal objects in recovered collections. Undertaken as a cultural resource management project during early 1990s, archaeological investigations in the central compound located three trash middens and one large trash pit, all associated with the demolition of the cotton factory in 1905. A total of 1,310 artifacts were recovered from the excavation of these penitentiary features (Wurtzburg and Hahn 1992a: 91). Ceramics primarily represented utilitarian vessels associated with sanitation activities, kitchen preparation and storage of bulk foods, and hospital treatment and storage of medicines. At least thirteen large stoneware jugs dating from 1880 to 1910 were recovered from the trash pit (Wurtzburg and Hahn 1992b: 27). With three of these two-gallon jugs bearing the mark of New Orleans wholesale druggist I. L. Lyons & Co., this assemblage was likely a result of the institution's dominant function as a repository for sick and depleted convicts rejected by the convict leasing system.

In contrast with collections from other places of institutional confinement discussed in this chapter, the ceramic assemblage from the Baton Rouge site contained few tablewares. Instead, several tin-enameled cups, bowls, and pans were recovered from excavation trenches (Wurtzburg and Hahn 1992b: 32). While philanthropic donations of used ceramic tablewares may have routinely supported other American institutions, the more fortunate citizens of Louisiana may not have extended similar charity to the predominantly African-American residents of the Old Baton Rouge Penitentiary. Conversely, since the four excavated trash features were linked to demolition activities of 1905, the dominant presence of tin-enameled tablewares may indicate the twentieth-century emergence of these commodities as a durable and cost-effective alternative to ceramics. In other words, the minimal living conditions of this Southern penitentiary may well reflect an overriding desire for fiscal conservatism rather than any philosophical ideology for social reform.

Excavations recovered a particularly high concentration of artifacts related to industrial production. Throughout the operations of the penitentiary, male inmates awaiting private contract assignment were employed at leatherwork and tailoring, creating institutional uniforms for internal distribution among both male and female convicts (Nobles 2000: 8). Assemblages recovered from the midden adjacent to the northern wing (trash midden 1) predominantly consisted of scrap leather related to the production of shoes and hats (Wurtzburg and Hahn 1992b: 39). Although most elements of the inmate uniform were produced by hand, approximately 100 steam-powered, belt-driven sewing machines were installed in the cotton factory during the late nineteenth century to speed production times. Portions of twenty-four of these sewing machines were recovered from the large trash pit, eight of which were manufactured by the Wheeler & Wilson Manufacturing Company of Bridgeport, Connecticut, and ten others by the Singer Manufacturing Company of New York (Wurtzburg and Hahn 1992b: 35).

What few personal items were archaeologically recovered suggest a clandestine maintenance of both illicit activities and inmate social networks in this place of austere confinement. Reminiscent of the bone artifacts recovered from the late eighteenth-century Walnut Street Prison, a single hand-carved bone die was found during excavation of trash midden 2, located near the north wing of the penitentiary compound. As an activity simultaneously associated with entertainment and exchange, dice gambling may have articulated with networks of black market or "sub rosa" trade (Casella 2002; V. L. Williams and Fish 1974; see chapter 3). Indeed, a substantial quantity of alcohol vessels, including liquor flasks in addition to wine and champagne bottles, appeared in glass assemblages. A particularly high concentration of these contraband objects were recovered from the excavated well feature, its inconspicuous location perhaps indicating covert acts of deposition (Wurtzburg and Hahn 1992b: 29).

Reflecting the growing interest in a diversity of carceral experiences, the institutional presence of both women and children at the Old Baton Rouge Penitentiary has been examined through a range of interdisciplinary scholarship (Tonry and Petersilia 2000; Howe 1994; Rafter 1990). Photographic evidence demonstrates a peripheral yet continuous record of both groups at the penitentiary. Artifact collections offer similar hints, with the leather assemblage retrieved from trash midden 1 containing at least one example of a child's shoe amid the general manufacture debris. A general notion of accelerated female incarceration over the decade following the Civil War—an assumption possibly linked to the increasing confinement of previously enslaved African-American men—has been disproved by feminist historical research. In actual fact, throughout the nineteenth century, women (both white and African-American) never constituted less than 5 percent of the total inmate population at the Old Baton Rouge Penitentiary—a ratio comparable to national figures generated during the 1980s (Fisher-Giorlando 1995: 24). Thus, the early twentieth-century establishment of separate female facilities may have had less to do with population increases than with broader changes in sentiment over the confinement of women (Rafter 1990). By 1908, during the final decade of the Baton Rouge penitentiary, the former "gin room" (which had probably housed cotton gin equipment) was transformed into a female cell block, with access to the facility provided through the eastern wall of the men's lower cell house (Wurtzburg and Hahn 1992b: 16).

While this separate accommodation improved security and sanitation arrangements for female convicts and their children, the penitentiary was already earmarked for closure and replacement. Though the Old Baton Rouge Penitentiary continued as a receiving station for new convicts through 1917, the great majority of convicts were relocated to the Angola Plantation Prison Farm to serve out their sentences. By 1918, all institutional structures at the old facility had been sold or dismantled. Thus, as the penitentiary template spread across America, an underlying tension over the purpose of confinement continued to dominate architectural designs (Friedman 1993; Wurtzburg and Hahn 1992a; Hauff 1988). Were the new institutions intended to maximize rehabilitative confinement or industrial production? With the emergence of federal maximum security incarceration at the turn of the century, this question achieved a temporary resolution.

Alcatraz Island (California)

Its notoriety peaking during the twentieth century, Alcatraz Island was originally developed as a U.S. military base during the second half of the nineteenth century. Located directly west of the Golden Gate, the island offered a valuable strategic site for defensive protection of the entrance to San Francisco Bay. During 1853, U.S. military engineers first began to fortify the island. A belt of stone and brick fortifications ringed the island by 1857, mounting a total of seventy-five guns over a total of eight separate batteries (Thompson 1979: 91–103). At the summit of the eastern hill, a permanent brick citadel for 200 men was completed by 1859 (Thompson 1979: 76). Major earthworks continued after the Civil War, with a parade ground, artificial slopes, and decorative gardens added to the compound over the 1870s.

Although the garrison had provided facilities for confinement of military prisoners since the Civil War, Alcatraz Island served increasingly as the primary west coast military prison, gaining particular importance in 1898 following the Spanish American War. From 1907 through 1933, the island officially operated as a United States Military Prison. When an upgraded facility for incarceration was federally funded, the original citadel was demolished to ground level between 1909 and 1912. Constructed of reinforced concrete, this new penitentiary provided incarceration for a maximum of 600 men. The central wing of the massive three-story cell block consisted of two floors. The basement, which recycled major elements of the original 1859 citadel brick arch support system, housed the administrative offices, storage rooms, and the inmate shower block. Containing three free-standing steel and concrete cell towers (blocks A through C), the first floor additionally housed the solitary confinement unit (block D), the library, visitors area, and main entrance control room. The kitchen and dining hall occupied a second wing, conjoined on the western side of the main cell block. While an oil-powered lighthouse had stood on Alcatraz since 1854, a new 84-foot reinforced concrete electrified lighthouse was added directly south of the main entrance to the cell block during the site renovations of 1909, thereby completing the primary structural landscape of this infamous penal compound.

The chilly bay climate, harsh disciplinary conditions, and visual prominence of Alcatraz conspired to create a popular image of the institution as "Uncle Sam's Devil's Island" (Delgado 1991: 22–27). Faced with mounting operational costs, in addition to growing civic and political disapproval, the U.S. Army decided to close its prison in 1932. Alcatraz Island transferred to the Bureau of

Prisons, transforming into the sixth facility in an expanding network of federal penitentiaries. The main cell block was immediately remodeled to enforce standards of maximum security. Tool-proof steel fronts and doors were added to the cell blocks and steel bars attached to windows and ventilation ducts. Two gun galleries, tear gas equipment, and new locking devices were installed in the main gallery (Thompson 1979: 500).

By 1936, a series of massive concrete steps were added to the eastern side of the parade ground, by then renamed the "recreation yard" (National Park Service 1993). A library and an isolation block of dark cells were added to the western side of the monumental cell block during 1939 and 1940. The island's power plant was also overhauled in 1940, with a steam turbine, a diesel engine, saltwater pumps, waterlines, steam lines, and fuel oil lines installed. The industrial buildings continued to house a rubber mat factory, tailor shop, shoe shop, wood shop, and furniture reconditioning shop.

By 1940, the Bureau of Prisons completed its final modifications on Alcatraz Island. Surveillance and confinement facilities were upgraded and modernized through the introduction of extensive security fences and six free-standing guard towers across the penal compound. To accommodate the growing number of correctional officers and administrators, a series of detached staff houses and three multistoried apartments were constructed over the former parade grounds on the eastern side of the island. While several of the military buildings were demolished, others were recycled or renovated. Towering over the Alcatraz Wharf, the four-story Building 64 Apartments, for example, retained foundations and a ground floor adapted from the original 1860s brick army barracks. These features survive today as some of the earliest architecture on the island (figure 4.1).

Since no natural freshwater source existed, a 250,000-gallon steel water tank was erected in 1939. This water not only served inmates and staff, but also the industrial laundry and the Model Industries Building on the western side of the penal compound. Although similar to the workshops of both the Walnut Street Prison and Old Rhode Island Penitentiary over a century earlier, these two facilities were never expected to generate enough profit to ensure complete financial sustainability. While mitigating operational costs, the Alcatraz industries were primarily intended to provide inmates with vocational training in manual skills. Operating for twenty-nine years before it closed in 1963, Alcatraz Island Federal Penitentiary gained infamy as a national emblem of American institutional confinement.

Following closure of the penitentiary, the island attracted media attention when Native American activists occupied it in November 1969, demanding land rights, educational support, and the establishment of a Native American

Figure 4.1. Wharf, Alcatraz Island Federal Penitentiary, California. Photograph depicts nineteenth-century structures: Building 64 (left) and sally port (white building, center); guard tower installed by Federal Bureau of Prisons in 1940. (Courtesy of Golden Gate National Recreational Area, Park Archives [GGNRA/PARC, Mary M. Bowman Photographic Collection].)

cultural center. The activists endured difficult living conditions and internal factional politics for nineteen months (Odier 1982: 229–39) until California governor Ronald Reagan ordered water and electricity supplies to the island shut down in 1971. As a result, the remaining Indian activists were peacefully escorted from the island by federal marshals. Since this controversial occupation exerted a profound influence over Native American politics, Alcatraz Island has emerged as an enduring symbol of indigenous activism.

With the establishment of the Golden Gate National Recreational Area by President Nixon, the island was opened to the public in October 1973. Serving as one of the premier tourist venues for the San Francisco region, Alcatraz is currently managed as a National Historic Landmark by the National Park Service. As a consequence of high visitor numbers, health and safety concerns, and the exposed location of the island, archaeological works over the past three decades have primarily involved the maintenance, restoration, and cultural heritage management of standing historic structures.

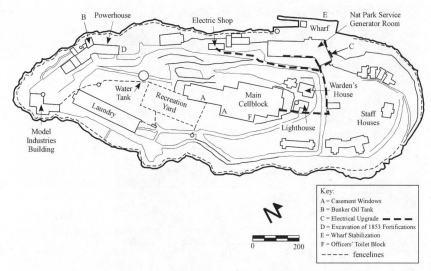

Figure 4.2. Plan of heritage works, Alcatraz Island, California. (Drawing by Eleanor Casella.)

Architectural monitoring and evaluation first commenced during the island's tenure as a federal penitentiary. In 1961, the Bureau of Prisons commissioned an extensive survey of structural conditions under the massive cell block building, particularly focused on remnants of the brick arch supports recycled from the original 1859 citadel. This survey documented a critical, extensive, and progressive deterioration of concrete floor slabs and steel support beams throughout the cell block basement. The dramatic estimate of $5 million to make these essential repairs hastened the close of the penitentiary only two years later (Thompson 1979: 413).

Since its transfer to the National Park Service, Alcatraz Island has undergone five major works projects designed to manage the historic built environment (Martin Mayer, Park Archaeologist, personal communications, 2002). With the western wall of the cell block directly exposed to the salt winds and damp fogs of the Golden Gate mouth of San Francisco Bay, severe erosion had permanently damaged the steel casements and glass windows lining that side of the building (figure 4.2). Similar problems beset the original glass skylights roofs that illuminated the two main internal corridors of the cell block (figure 4.3). Thus, the first major heritage project on Alcatraz Island involved the weatherization of these historic features, with archaeologists monitoring the removal, cleaning, and replacement of all structural elements over two project phases: 1977 to 1978 and 1985 to 1986.

Figure 4.3. Skylights above "Broadway Street" between cell blocks C and B, Alcatraz Island Federal Penitentiary, California. (Library of Congress, Historic American Buildings Survey-California [HABS CAL, 38-ALCA, 1-A-21].)

A similar building maintenance project was undertaken during 1978–79 when the bunker oil tank on the northeastern edge of the island began to leak residual oil into the San Francisco Bay (see figure 4.2). Originally constructed in 1873 as a powder magazine, the structure had been modified in 1937 to contain the heavy diesel oil used for the island's electric generator. The potential presence of nineteenth-century artifacts required archaeological monitoring during both the retrieval of the remaining bunker oil and the cleaning of the brick structure. Nonetheless, only one miniature steel anvil was recovered from the oil sludge deposited inside the tank.

A major upgrade of the island's electrical system was undertaken during 1986–87 (see figure 4.2). As part of these works, the original 1912 steam turbine direct-current generators in the powerhouse (Building 67) were replaced by three new diesel generators installed in a new electrical facility on the wharf.

Following archaeological advice, the route of the original distribution system was replicated. New conduit and cable wires were installed from the wharf up to the lighthouse and across to the main entrance of the cell block. By maintaining the historic distribution route, impacts to both the standing historic structures and intact subsurface deposits were strategically minimized.

Because of the dense and multiphased occupation of Alcatraz Island, structural assessments have frequently resulted in the retrieval of archaeological remains. During July 1998, archaeological excavations were undertaken at the quartermaster's storehouse (Building 79) as part of a survey of geologic stability on the northeastern side of the island (see figure 4.2). The test trench revealed foundations of the original 1850s brick and stone fortifications, with two separate construction periods represented in changes to the building materials. Similarly, a seismic rehabilitation of the wharf and landing dock was completed during 2001 to mitigate the effects of saltwater erosion (see figure 4.2). During replacement of the rotten wooden piles and support beams, samples were retrieved for analysis and compared with historic accounts. The archaeological results link the current wharf to Bureau of Prison improvements of the late 1930s rather than to the earlier late nineteenth-century wooden structure.

Following transfer of Alcatraz Island to the National Park Service, a small collection of artifacts associated with the federal penitentiary were recovered by park rangers from the officer's toilet area in the southwest corner of the cell block (see figure 4.2). Retrieved in the late 1970s as zones of the prison were prepared for public visitors, the collection included materials associated with everyday inmate life, including a metal-alloy spoon, a yellow plastic toothbrush, a pressed ferrous-metal meal tray, and assorted brown glass aspirin bottles. Prison industrial activities were also represented, including a black rubber sole from a U.S. Army boot, an object related to military contracts fulfilled in the model industries building.

A few intriguing artifacts were recovered, hinting at insubordination in the penitentiary. These included a large ferrous serving spoon, its bowl flattened and sharpened at the edge, and a metal-alloy fork, its tines twisted into a lock pick. Displaying a series of cuts along its handle, one metal-alloy teaspoon in the Alcatraz collection had been partially modified into a skeleton key (figure 4.4). As subversive objects, these artifacts offered a hidden transcript of anonymous activities that inevitably accumulated into broader patterns of collective inmate resistance (Scott 1990; B. Morris 1988; see chapter 3).

Thus, archaeological projects at Alcatraz illuminate the fundamental evolution in design, function, and internal organization that has transformed carceral experience over the last two centuries. From the late eighteenth-century prisons of the New Republic through the concrete palaces of the twentieth

Figure 4.4. Metal-alloy teaspoon, Alcatraz Island Collection, National Park Service, Golden Gate National Recreational Area. (Photograph by Eleanor Casella.)

century, institutions of punishment have functioned as places of disciplinary control, unfree labor, circumstantial power, moral reform, and everyday insubordination. Serving as a mode of punishment, institutional confinement has thereby defined a unique material relationship between the American state and its citizenry. This chapter will now turn to examine how similar themes arise when institutional confinement is applied as a mode of social welfare.

Confinement as Asylum

From the seventeenth through the nineteenth century, places of confinement were established across the nation to accommodate destitute and unproductive citizens. Archaeological research offers new diachronic perspectives on the application of institutional confinement to dependent members of American society. These material studies coalesce around three major themes, exploring how changing labor relations, basic living conditions, and ritual practices guided the experience of daily life within institutions of asylum.

Devil's Currency: Industry, Labor, and the Almshouse

From its origins, the underlying aims of the workhouse involved promotion of productive industry—a relationship extensively theorized by both Marxist criminologists (Melossi and Pavarini 1981; Rusche and Kirchheimer 1968) and revisionist historians (Foucault 2001 [1964]; Christianson 1998; Katz 1986; Ignatieff 1978). Consequently, archaeologists have explored material implications of labor regimes in institutions of asylum. As new demands for productivity articulated with basic character assessments of those in need, American almshouses began to discriminate between the "deserving" and the "undeserving" or "vagabond" poor (Spencer-Wood and Baugher 2001). Thus, from the earliest colonial period, American institutions operated as subsidized places of industry with inmates producing valued commodities for both external sale and internal consumption.

The Albany Almshouse (New York)

Founded by the Dutch Reform Church in 1684, the Albany Almshouse was first established to serve paupers from the Dutch colony of Fort Orange. This continental influence was to have a substantial impact on the organization and operation of this early American asylum. Although the New Netherland colonial territories were ceded to the British government in 1664, a distinctively Dutch culture and social structure persisted over the eighteenth century throughout the region (Huey 2001; also see chapter 2). A key element of this cultural influence was apparent in the organization of poor relief. In contrast with English ideas, traditional Dutch notions of public charity defined the management and distribution of poor relief as a congregational responsibility, one firmly vested within the Dutch Reform Church rather than in secular authorities. To achieve the prestigious social qualities of *deftigheid* (or dignity and stateliness) the Dutch burgher (or middle-class citizen) openly embraced civic responsibilities toward the less fortunate (Peña 2001: 157). As a result, in the former colonies of New Netherland, the mobilization of donations and material support for poor relief straddled both ecclesiastical and secular realms of society.

Since alms recipients were expected to aspire toward self-sufficiency, various work programs were established within charitable institutions of the seventeenth and eighteenth centuries. Archaeological evidence indicates that the specific industry adopted at Albany's almshouse involved the manufacture of a distinctly North American commercial product: wampum. Made from both local and imported hard sea shells, the most common raw materials were coastal clams (*Mercenaria mercenaria*) from New York or conch (*Stigas strombus*) imported from the Dutch colony of Curaçao (L. Williams and Flinn 1990: 29), although other Caribbean species have been archaeologically recovered (figure 4.5). With a variety of craft tools, shells were ground and polished into both white and purple beads for exchange, either as loose product or by the fathom—a 6-foot length of strung beads. With approximately five beads to an inch, the average fathom consisted of 360 beads.

After its rejection as "devil's currency" by some eighteenth-century English colonists, wampum no longer served as legal tender in the region (Peña 2001: 159). Nonetheless, the product continued to provide a central means of exchange between Albany merchants and fur traders of the northern Canadian frontier. Specific values were attached to wampum, and fathoms could be exchanged for both Dutch and English currency. Thus, in the American colonial

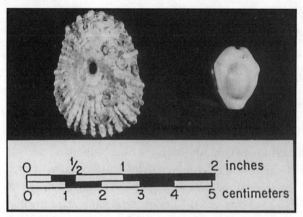

Figure 4.5. Cowrie shell and Barbadian keyhole limpet shell, Albany Almshouse, New York. (Joseph McEvoy photograph provided by Elizabeth Peña, courtesy of the New York State Museum, Albany.)

context, wampum served as a valuable product for the Albany Almshouse. While participating in this economically pragmatic labor regime, the impoverished residents were literally manufacturing money.

Excavations in the northern half of the Albany Almshouse building revealed a series of stratigraphic contexts which, dated on the basis of recovered ceramic evidence, span the late seventeenth and mid-eighteenth centuries. Shell artifacts recovered from these soil layers demonstrate the site was a central locus of wampum production. Beads, blanks, and raw shell material in all stages of production were collected. The resulting assemblage illuminated the craft technology required to create wampum, with various methods of shaping, drilling, and polishing represented. Production tools such as whetstones and iron drills were also located within deposits (Peña 2001: 164). As testimony to the delicate skills involved in manufacture, considerable wastage was recovered, primarily due to the tendency of the shells to split during the drilling of the central hole. Of the forty-nine unfinished beads recovered, almost 47 percent had been drilled from one end and split, 20.4 percent had split after completion of drilling, and 12.2 percent had been drilled from both ends before splitting (Peña 2001: 169).

From a broader socioeconomic perspective, the archaeological presence of wampum production linked the labor regimes of early institutions to the broader emergence of modern commodity relations. The destitute underclass of colonial Albany crafted wampum because the beads were economically useful: they could be sold for legal currency rather than operating as money in themselves. Thus, the labor regime of this eighteenth-century almshouse offers an early American example of protoindustrialization. By shifting inmates from production for local consumption to standardized production for an external market, the Albany Almshouse introduced a pivotal component of the new industrial economy into the charitable institution. Further, wampum manufacture represented an early extension of capitalist entrepreneurial activity into the institutional management of vulnerable groups of Americans. Historical accounts suggest a tight arrangement of public and private partnership existed between almshouse administrators and local merchants for distribution and exchange of the finished wampum (Peña 2001: 171). Through this privatized system, the Dutch Reformed Church received financial assistance toward the cost of poor relief, while simultaneously providing a profit for local middlemen traders. Thus, through the basic organization of its economy, the Albany Almshouse brought the civic administration of poor relief into the revolutionary grasp of modern capitalism.

The Uxbridge Almshouse (Massachusetts)

Founded by the Town of Uxbridge, this public almshouse in Worcester County, Massachusetts, operated as a poor farm, providing a combination of subsidized domestic and agricultural labor for indigent men, women, and families from the local parish. Located on the southeastern edge of the township, the Uxbridge Almshouse operated between 1831 and 1872, accommodating a population that ranged from forty-three inmates in 1837 to nine in 1860 (Cook 1991: 66). Rediscovery and excavation of the Uxbridge Almshouse Burial Ground, undertaken as part of a highway project in the 1980s, enabled archaeologists to examine the osteological and pathological impacts of labor regimes within nineteenth-century institutions of asylum. This research thereby illuminated the forensic legacy of those embodied practices that literally shaped asylum inhabitants (De Cunzo 2006; Howe 1994; Butler 1993; Foucault 1977).

A total of thirty-two individuals—twenty-four adults, seven children, and one of indeterminate age—were exhumed from thirty-one graves. Evidence of a childbirth tragedy was present, with the one double inhumation (grave 27) containing the skeletons of a young woman and neonate (Elia 1991: 284). An arthritis-like condition of the spinal column was identified in eight adults, occurring in individuals who were forty to fifty or more years old at death (Elia 1991: 285). Consistent with the aging process, this pathological condition also indicates the distinct presence of elders from the parish in the asylum. In general, the mortality profile from the Uxbridge Almshouse Burial Ground matches historical demographic profiles of institutional populations, with a disproportionately high representation of elderly individuals present—48 percent of adult graves—when compared with profiles from noninstitutional cemeteries. Similar institutional mortality patterns have been recorded from excavations at the Highland Park poorhouse cemetery of western New York State and the early postmedieval hospital cemetery of St. James and St. Mary Magdalene of Chichester, southern England (Roberts et al. 1998; Lanphear 1988). Census data on the Uxbridge Almshouse taken from 1850 through 1865 supports this demographic profile, with single elderly women and men constituting more than 34 percent of the total asylum population over the fifteen-year period (Cook 1991: 67). Taken together, these interdisciplinary sources provide an image of the almshouse as a place of institutional confinement for isolated and vulnerable elders of the local parish community.

Osteological analysis also discovered a number of pathological conditions that may represent work conditions in the asylum. Lesions identified in the spinal vertebrae of three adults resulted either from years of strenuous activity or from short episodes of heavy lifting. Osteitis or inflammation of the bone was recorded in six adults, mostly occurring in their legs. Fractures were noted on the jaw of one inmate, on the foot of two inmates and, in the case of grave 17, on the hip, knee, foot, and finger of one particularly unfortunate inmate (Wesolowsky 1991: 244). These injuries and inflammations appear consistent with lively outdoor work or extensive walking—exactly the kind of agricultural work required of inmates at the Uxbridge Poor Farm. With gendered relations institutionally enforced, the taskwork assigned to male paupers included "clearing, manuring, and plowing of fields, planting, mowing, and bailing of hay, harvesting of other crops, threshing, slaughtering, and maintenance of the farm and its buildings" (Cook 1991: 71). Other male activities involved timber harvesting—a demanding operation in terms of both energy expenditure and injury risks. Additional dairying, livestock tending, and gardening duties were typically assigned to female inmates.

This agrarian mode of labor was common throughout nineteenth-century institutions, with a variety of hospitals, prisons, and asylums promoting farm work as a bucolic instrument for both medical therapy and moral rehabilitation. Administrators, such as the board of trustees at the Michigan State Mental Hospital, appreciated not only the improvements in inmate health, but also the economic benefits derived from agricultural surpluses produced on the institutional farms (Becker and Nassaney 2005). As institutional confinement increasingly relocated to suburban and rural settings over the nineteenth century, property holdings associated with these institutions frequently included the equipment, livestock, and agricultural fields required to support this agrarian mode of labor.

As the Albany and Uxbridge case studies demonstrate, archaeological research has illuminated two contrasting modes of labor in American institutions of asylum. While the Dutch Reform Church embraced new forms of capitalist and protoindustrial production at its eighteenth-century asylum in Albany, civic leaders in Uxbridge adopted a more traditional agrarian approach over a century later. Emphasizing labor-intensive over capital-intensive forms of labor, the Uxbridge Town Farm was designed to channel inmates toward self-sufficiency rather than explicit profit-generating industry.

By Frugal Means: Living Conditions within the Almshouse

Having considered institutional labor—the first of three main themes that inform material studies of asylums—we turn to the second: the living conditions experienced by inmates. Did institutional confinement provide a comfortable, if communal, variant of domestic life? Or did inmates suffer brutal and inhumane conditions? Archaeology offers fresh material perspectives on the qualitative nature of daily life in these institutions.

The New York City Almshouse

Founded in 1736 as New York City's first municipal asylum, by the time it closed in 1797, the charitable complex had expanded to include three major structures and a number of associated outbuildings. Located at the southern end of Manhattan Island and accommodating up to 425 inmates, the site served as both a house of correction for the able-bodied poor and as a shelter for the sick, disabled, and elderly. The design of the main compound followed a typical rectilinear pattern with the central building flanked by separate kitchen and hospital facilities (Baugher and Lenik 1997: 8). In common with both the Uxbridge Asylum and Michigan State Mental Hospital, the New York City Almshouse supported a range of agricultural industries throughout its gardens, orchards, and grazing fields. Documentary evidence indicates that an additional range of domestic industries operated there, including sewing, spinning, laundering, cooking, baking, childcare, and picking oakum—a repetitive task involving the stripping of salt- and tar-encrusted ropes discarded from ships to recycle the hemp fibers as boat caulking (Baugher 2001: 184).

Excavations undertaken during the late 1980s uncovered stone foundations and stratified deposits associated with an eighteenth-century building from the almshouse complex (figure 4.6). Identified as a brick and stone kitchen structure added to the compound in 1736, the demolished remains contained a layer of loose soil, plaster, and whitewash above the floor of the original basement (Baugher and Lenik 1997). A total of 1,037 artifacts and 876 faunal remains were recovered from this kitchen deposit (Baugher 2001: 178). When subjected to detailed analysis, these material assemblages raised new questions about the nature of life in this eighteenth-century municipal institution. Despite histori-

Figure 4.6. Stratigraphic profile of material inside the basement of the New York City Almshouse kitchen. (Photograph by F. A. Winter and H. A. Bankoff, Brooklyn College, CUNY.)

cal portrayals of the asylum as a brutal environment of discipline and deprivation (Ross 1988; McCartney 1987; Katz 1986), archaeological evidence suggests
a more humane set of living conditions prevailed within the New York City
Almshouse than was previously thought.

Children admitted to the almshouse constituted almost 30 percent of the
residents over its decades of operation (Baugher 2001: 190). A number of
colonial churches sponsored charity schools to provide free education and
vocational training for juvenile paupers. The content of these philanthropic
programs remained firmly gendered, with boys taught reading, writing, and
arithmetic, and girls instructed in sewing and knitting (Katz 1986: 118–21; Mohl
1971: 175–76). To this strict document-based image of childhood under institutional confinement, archaeological work has contributed evidence of a more
whimsical set of inmate activities. A total of ten artifacts classified as toys were
recovered from kitchen deposits. Consisting of six clay marbles, three stone
marbles, and one small indented clay ball, these artifacts suggest that games
and social play enhanced daily life in the almshouse (Baugher 2001: 190).

Other assemblages similarly demonstrated a more humane vision of living conditions in the institution. With 83 percent of the ceramic assemblage
consisting of decorated artifacts (including hand-painted and transfer-printed
creamwares, shell-edged pearlwares, scratch-blue stonewares, and tin-glazed
delftwares), the New York City Almshouse appeared to have been provisioned
with diverse and unmatched, yet still fashionable dishes mirroring those of
middle- and upper-class tables throughout the city (Baugher 2001: 186). Approximately 18 percent of the tablewares represented tea services, with an
engine-turned stoneware teapot fragment recovered in addition to Chinese
export porcelain, creamware, and hand-painted pearlware cups. The presence
of such ceramics in the almshouse may reflect patterns of philanthropic donation, with urban consumers gifting unmatched pieces as they replaced and upgraded their dinner sets. Perhaps, in a material reflection of New York's Dutch
colonial origins, a residual continental spirit of civic responsibility encouraged
the good burghers of the city to maintain hospitable living standards within
their municipal asylum. Certainly the faunal remains recovered from kitchen
deposits indicate a frugal, yet fully adequate, diet was provided during confinement, with the remains of cattle, caprines (sheep and goats), pigs, chickens, fish
and shellfish represented in the collections (Baugher 2001: 187).

Humane institutional conditions were interpreted from a final group of artifacts recovered from the New York City Almshouse. While historical accounts
suggest the increasing imposition of distinguishing uniforms and badges in
poor relief schemes of the eighteenth century (Ross 1988: 152–53; McCartney
1987: 292), materials recovered from kitchen deposits contained no examples

of this particular disciplinary mechanism. Rather, clothing ornaments and fasteners suggest that individual expression, health and well-being, diversity, and freedom of choice were maintained through inmate appearance. These assemblages contained forty-four buttons, demonstrating a wide variety of styles that ranged from gilded or stamped copper-alloy shanked buttons, to simple sew-through bone buttons. Other artifactual materials indicate that almshouse residents manufactured clothing, either for personal use or commercial sale. Approximately forty-seven copper-alloy straight pins were recovered from the kitchen deposits. Further, the button assemblage contained approximately seventy-six bone blanks and fragments of bone button debitage, with a number of these artifacts exhibiting metal manufacture cuts (Baugher 2001: 189).

Thus, material assemblages from the New York City Almshouse kitchen suggest that, at least in the original Dutch colonies, a charitable attitude toward the deserving poor may have prevailed over the eighteenth century (Huey 2001). As detailed in chapter 2, the mid-eighteenth-century almshouses of English colonies such as Virginia and Massachusetts were intended to function as self-supporting, if not profit-generating, institutions of asylum. This expectation yielded the far more utilitarian facilities and resources provided within their walls (McCartney 1987; Katz 1986). Although residents of the New York City Almshouse lived under frugal conditions, these urban inmates received a varied and nutritionally adequate diet, maintained a sense of individuality, and enjoyed leisure and family activities. Their surrounding material world did not suggest a stark institutional environment. Significantly, this image of a modest yet humane existence has also emerged from archaeological work on asylums of the following century.

The Old Poor House of Falmouth (Massachusetts)

Originally constructed in 1769 as a crossroads tavern, the weatherboard two-story building was purchased in 1812 by the Falmouth village of southeastern Massachusetts. Relocated to its present site by 1814, the structure underwent major renovations during 1823 when it was converted into a new poor house intended to accommodate a maximum of thirty inmates (Strauss and Spencer-Wood 1999: 31, 41). Operating until 1920, the weatherboard building was transferred to the Falmouth Artists Guild during the early 1960s. The site underwent extensive structural survey and archaeological testing during the late 1990s in preparation for access and drainage works proposed for the building exterior. Results of these studies provided new perspectives on living conditions in this nineteenth-century asylum.

Architectural evidence collected during the building survey suggests an increasing adoption of disciplinary mechanism over the early years of operation.

Figure 4.7. Eastern interior, second floor of the Falmouth Almshouse, showing three doors. The right door led into a hall without windows, while the central and left doors let into 8-by-8-foot rooms. Original wide floor boards (laid east to west) were retained on the second floor in addition to wide-board wainscoting. (Photograph by Suzanne Spencer-Wood.)

Town records from 1824 indicate that the two main stories and attic of the almshouse were subdivided into twenty-four separate cubicles, each measuring 8 by 8 feet (2.4 by 2.4 m.). Surviving remnants of these rooms, including vestigial doorways and floorboard patterns (figure 4.7), suggest the room divisions were added to the preexisting building, as the interior layout seemed too awkward to represent an original integral design (Strauss and Spencer-Wood 1999: 34).

Intended for an individual occupant, each room was large enough to contain a single cot and dresser. These structural modifications may demonstrate a dramatic shift "from the family-style congregate living methods of care used in the eighteenth century, to increasing use of nineteenth century . . . methods of creating an orderly institution by classifying and segregating inmates" (Strauss and Spencer-Wood 1999: 33; see also Lucas 1999; Foucault 1977; and chapter 3). Records show a total of seventeen paupers were admitted to the Falmouth Poor House in 1824, their separation into solitary rooms increasing administrative control over any unruly or disordered behaviors. Indeed, town records from the early 1840s document public funding for additional on-site accommodation. This new building was explicitly intended to improve confinement of "the refractory and unmanageable" and enable separation of the insane from the general population of inmates (Strauss and Spencer-Wood 1999: 40). Conversely, separate rooms also enhanced privacy and personal security in the asylum. Alms recipients may have actually appreciated a solitary alternative to both the dormitory-style accommodation previously available and to the overcrowded conditions that characterized underclass life in nineteenth-century America.

In any case, artifacts associated with the Falmouth Poor House suggest that residents enjoyed humane, if frugal, living conditions under nineteenth-century institutional confinement. A diverse variety of materials were recovered from excavation trenches situated on all four exterior sides of the almshouse. Glass assemblages contained two patent medicine bottles embossed with "Davis Vegetable Painkiller," which suggests some degree of medical care (figure 4.8). Ceramics recovered from the lower stratigraphic layers displayed manufacture dates from the first decades of the nineteenth century and tended to consist of pearlwares. In contrast, upper layers, deposited as a result of mid-1890s earthworks, contained much higher frequencies of the whitewares and ironstone ceramics typical of nineteenth-century American consumer patterns (Strauss and Spencer-Wood 1999: 103). Excavated tablewares were generally interpreted as representing middle-class tastes—with transfer-printed, plain, and shell-edged pearlware dishes recovered along with banded and spongeware bowls, fragmentary Chinese export porcelains, and decorated pearlware tea service artifacts. No matched ceramic sets were recovered during excavations.

Two possible interpretations have been developed to account for the unusual age of this collection. First, since this mid-century assemblage was dominated by outdated pearlwares, the collection may represent charitable donations by more fortunate citizens of Falmouth—an argument that echoes interpretations from the New York City Almshouse project. However, documentary sources indicate that inmates frequently brought along personal possessions when admitted to the Falmouth Poor House. Particularly because recovered assemblages include a molded body fragment from a white porcelain figurine, archaeologists have raised the intriguing possibility that some of the older items in the ceramic collection may represent treasured objects, brought to the institution by destitute residents as melancholic or aspirational symbols of better times (Strauss and Spencer-Wood 1999: 109).

If these artifacts represent treasured memorabilia or family heirlooms, their presence suggests that certain personal possessions and material expressions of individual identity were permitted in the almshouse despite its enthusiastic adoption of other disciplinary mechanisms (such as solitary accommodation). Archaeological evidence may thus indicate that the Falmouth asylum operated

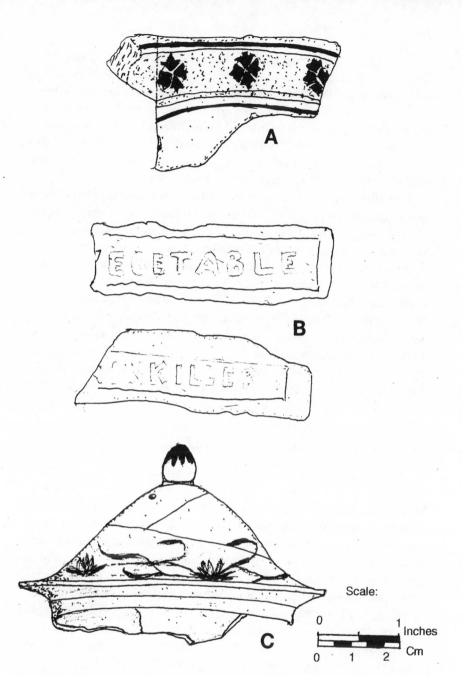

Figure 4.8. Artifacts recovered from the east rear yard of the Falmouth Almshouse. (A) Hand-painted pearlware tea bowl; (B) Davis Vegetable Painkiller clear glass medicine bottle; (C) hand-painted pearlware tea bowl lid. (Drawing by Suzanne Spencer-Wood.)

as more of a subsidized boardinghouse than a "total institution" (Goffman 1961; see chapter 3). In stark contrast with the structured dispossession, or "leaving off and taking on," that characterizes entry into the austere facility of Goffman's sociological study (1961: 18), material expressions of individual identity at the Falmouth Poor House can be inferred from artifacts related to personal appearance, such as a woman's tortoise shell comb and a wide variety of glass, copper-alloy, jet stone, wood, and iron buttons recovered from soil deposits predating the 1890s (Strauss and Spencer-Wood 1999: 109).

Regardless of whether the decorative tablewares and ornamental figurines arrived as personal possessions or charitable donations—or even belonged to the almshouse keeper and his family—the ubiquitous presence of pottery in excavated assemblages firmly demonstrates that almshouse inmates took their meals on ceramic dishes. Not, in other words, on the white enameled tinwares depicted in historical accounts as the norm for nineteenth-century American workhouses (Rothman 1990: 191). On the basis of findings generated at sites like the Falmouth Poor House, some scholars have concluded that the modest yet adequate living conditions established in eighteenth-century asylums continued into the subsequent century. Notwithstanding the humane image generated by these archaeological projects, almshouses always existed as places of confinement for vulnerable citizens relegated to the margins of society. Other studies of American almshouses offer a less favorable picture of living conditions in these charitable institutions.

The Smithfield Town Farm and Asylum (Rhode Island)

Similar to the Uxbridge Almshouse, the town farm and asylum of nineteenth-century Smithfield, Rhode Island, utilized agricultural labor as a mechanism for transforming the unproductive into the industrious. Accommodating up to thirty residents in a multistory dormitory, the Smithfield Asylum operated from 1834 through 1870, when a municipal inquest into accusations of starvation and inmate abuse resulted in closure of the facility and sale of its buildings and grounds (Garman and Russo 1999: 130–33).

Archaeological investigations undertaken during the early 1990s recovered stratigraphically sealed yard surface deposits on the northern, eastern, and western sides of the town farm dormitory foundations. A total of ninety-one ceramic vessels were collected from these nineteenth-century depositional contexts, representing tablewares, serving dishes, and hygiene vessels either purchased in unmatched lots or donated to the institution by more prosperous members of the township (Garman and Russo 1999: 127). While generally similar to other nineteenth-century collections, the Smithfield assemblage was primarily distinguished by its age. Analysis demonstrated a surprisingly high frequency of unmatched decorated pearlwares, with both transfer-printed (30 percent) and hand-painted (18 percent) variants represented within the assemblage. Undecorated and edge-molded creamwares constituted the second highest component of the asylum collection.

To demonstrate how obsolete the assemblage was during the institution's years of operation, a mean ceramic date of 1815.94 was derived from the total collection (Garman and Russo 1999: 128). This result suggests the town farm was supplied with ceramics that had survived two or more decades beyond their peak years of production. By 1835, when the institution began operation, middle-class American consumers had begun to enthusiastically replace pearlware table settings and serving vessels with new durable transfer-printed whitewares and ironstones (Wall 1994).

Echoing results from the New York City and Falmouth sites, the Town Farm ceramics were interpreted as discarded goods from the Smithfield community donated to the asylum as local middle-class consumers renewed and upgraded their household property. However, in contrast with the previous projects, archaeologists at the town farm site did not read the ceramic assemblage as a material signature of civic responsibility or community philanthropy. Their final interpretations, in fact, linked the dumping of obsolete ceramics to the charitable warehousing of the destitute and vulnerable within this public asylum (Garman and Russo 1999: 129).

The Cook County Poor Farm (Illinois)

Biocultural research also supports a rather stark perspective on living conditions in nineteenth-century institutions of asylum. Gender-linked patterns of morbidity and mortality were identified through a detailed analysis of human remains exhumed from a cemetery associated with the Cook County Poor Farm, Chicago's first municipal almshouse (Grauer et al. 1998). Also known as the Dunning Poorhouse, the institution operated from 1851 through 1869 on the western side of the city. Documentary accounts record that a maximum population of 435 inmates were accommodated within a three-story brick building and an adjacent two-story wing reserved for the insane.

Skeletons of poorhouse inmates were evaluated to determine the nature of stress in bone and dental materials. To differentiate childhood-related deficiencies from disease and trauma related to asylum conditions, a number of pathological conditions were examined. The presence of both porotic hyperostosis, a spongy appearance of the crania associated with childhood anemia, and linear enamel hypoplasia, an abnormal formation of tooth enamel caused by various childhood deficiencies, was used to gauge the health of asylum inmates upon institutional entry. In contrast, cavities, periodontitis (gum disease), bone trauma, and periostitis (skeletal lesions associated with systemic infection) were all linked to health, diet, and hygiene conditions at the Cook County Poor Farm.

Results of paleopathological research suggest that gender difference produced starkly divergent experiences of institutional confinement. Of the 120 individuals exhumed from the cemetery site, fifty-two could be assigned to both a sex category and an age-at-death interval (Grauer et al. 1998: 152). Both historical sources and skeletal evidence indicate that most asylum inmates were between twenty-five and thirty-five years of age. Documentary accounts further note a gender imbalance in the asylum, with males accounting for approximately 60 percent of the inmate population over the 1850s. The cemetery sample, however, does not reflect a similar pattern of male predominance. When demographic patterns were compared with paleopathological data, results suggested gender- and age-linked patterns of death in the nineteenth-century poorhouse. Accounting for only 40 percent of the living resident population, females constituted 52 percent of the total cemetery sample. Further, for those twenty-one individuals aged over thirty-five years, over 57 percent were females. Thus, while "more males entered the facility, a higher proportion of entering females never left" (Grauer et al. 1998: 156).

Disease and trauma impaired the lives of both men and women at the Cook County Poor Farm. Similar rates of injury, infection, and poor dental health impacted both groups. Females were as likely to have endured childhood anemia and developmental stress as male inmates. Nonetheless, examination of human remains exposed significant gender differences in the embodied experience of confinement (De Cunzo 2006; see chapter 3). Close documentary analysis demonstrates that healthy young men, while accounting for the majority of inmates, also comprised the greatest number of those discharged. Skeletal evidence demonstrates that a high proportion of those males who remained confined had experienced adverse childhood development conditions and, as a result, suffered poor health and dental disease upon institutional entry.

In contrast, women entered the asylum at younger ages than men and, once confined, tended to leave by death rather than institutional discharge. While typically in reasonable health at the time of their admittance, "they were dying of acute conditions contracted shortly before their deaths" (Grauer et al. 1998: 161). Additionally, a greater proportion of the older females exhumed from the cemetery site displayed pathologies. In other words, rather than being the result of chronic childhood conditions, it was prolonged institutional residence that disproportionately jeopardized their lives.

Taken together, the archaeological studies presented here offer a somewhat ambivalent image of living conditions in American almshouses. While the excavated artifact collections suggest that relatively humane, yet frugal, environments were maintained under institutional confinement, architectural and skeletal evidence demonstrate that an increasingly disciplinary and insalubrious experience gradually emerged over the nineteenth century. We turn now to consider how the material world operated on those confined within institutions of asylum.

Embodied Rituals: On the Practice of Everyday Life

How did inmates experience institutional confinement? By drawing information from the material record, archaeologists have begun to consider the ritual aspects of daily life in places of asylum. Exploring the symbolic roles of excavated assemblages, archaeological analysis has illuminated both transformational and subversive material encounters within the asylum. This research offers a compelling experiential perspective on the nature of social power, linking the emergence of a distinctive inmate consciousness to the materiality of confinement.

The Magdalen Asylum of Philadelphia (Pennsylvania)

Founded in 1800, the Magdalen Society of Philadelphia drew upon the organizational bylaws, religious models, and architectural plans of the mid-eighteenth-century Magdalen Charity of London to establish a new American institution dedicated to the temporary refuge of young, unmarried women. Designed, according to their 1802 act of incorporation, for "meliorating the distressed condition of those unhappy females who have been seduced from the paths of virtue, and are desirous of returning to a life of rectitude" (qtd. in De Cunzo 1995: 17–18), by 1807 the asylum encompassed 1.25 acres of land on the northwestern edge of Philadelphia.

The original asylum was a late eighteenth-century four-story brick tenant house purchased as part of the property lot. The first addition, a three-story brick building erected in 1809, provided additional accommodation, an infirmary, and a workroom for inmates to the rear of the structure. A damaging storm in 1842 prompted considerable alterations to the asylum. An insurance survey undertaken in 1857 noted the architectural embellishment of functionally specific spaces in the renovated asylum (figure 4.9). These included the rear workroom, kitchens, and thirteen separate accommodation chambers of 10 by 12 feet (3 by 3.7 m.) located on the second, third, and fourth floors of the Magdalen House (De Cunzo 1995: 39). Like all other nineteenth-century institutions, the Magdalen Asylum was designed to reform the soul of the inmate through the rehabilitative mechanism of productive labor. Thus, until its relocation and closure in 1915, the asylum provided daily training in domestic

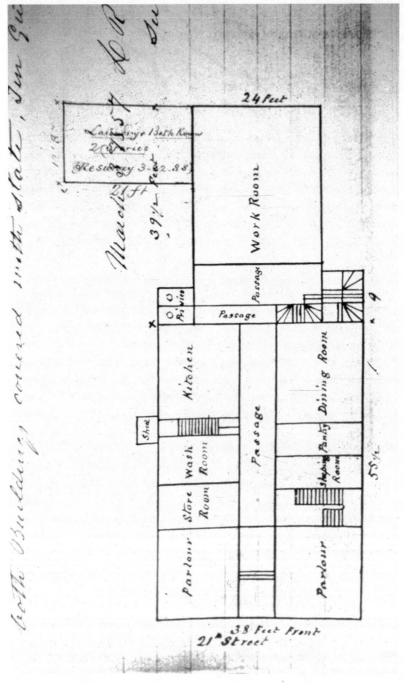

Figure 4.9. Insurance survey (1857), as amended, showing first-floor plan of the Magdalen Society Asylum, Philadelphia, Pennsylvania. (Reproduced by permission of the Philadelphia Contributionship for the Insurance of Houses from Loss by Fire.)

and laundry service as well as textile production to prepare female inmates for labor opportunities considered morally appropriate for women of the lower social orders.

How was reform materially enacted? Spatial isolation provided the principal mechanism for transforming inmates. From 1810, high wooden fences surrounded the asylum grounds, securing inmates from the moral temptations and unsavory socioeconomic networks of their former urban lives. Originally constructed of 8-foot (2.4 m.) timber paling surmounted by a row of spikes, the fencing was replaced in 1842 by a substantial perimeter wall of brick and dressed stone approximately 13 feet (4 m.) high and 14 inches (35.6 cm.) thick (De Cunzo 1995: 81). This boundary wall enclosed asylum facilities, including a series of segregated exercise yards subdivided by rows of internal wooden fences. Near the asylum house, hired male gardeners maintained large floral and vegetable garden beds interlaced with paved pathways and fruit trees. Archaeological research interpreted these garden features as an ideological landscape, the cultivation of tame nature intended as a visual (if highly contested) metaphor for the domesticated serenity of asylum inmates (De Cunzo 1995: 86–87).

Within this isolated environment, women performed a daily routine that demanded their constant personal engagement with the institution. Drawing from anthropological theories of "ritual practice" (Bell 1992; Turner 1969; Douglas 1966), Lu Ann De Cunzo has explored the material world of the Magdalen Asylum as a "liminal space"—a realm created for the rejection, transformation, and final reintegration of the inmate's self-identity. Upon admission to the asylum, women underwent specific rites of passage marking their entry into institutional confinement. While escorted to the matron's chamber deep within the Magdalen House, the inmate passed through five doorways to reach the office—an architectural metaphor for social withdrawal from her previous life. Inside the office, the inmate's clothes and personal belongings were removed and replaced by the asylum uniform. She was then issued a consecutive institutional entry number, which would henceforth serve as her ritual name during incarceration. The inmate was assigned a solitary bedchamber, the isolated confessional space intended to cultivate her moral rehabilitation. From that moment on, her daily routine of meals, prayer, domestic tasks, exercise, sewing, and laundry was institutionally regulated (De Cunzo 1995: 119). From the early 1830s, these basic rites of passage were elaborated to include a unique spatial classification of new arrivals. With the construction of a separate accommodation ward connected to the main house by a rear passageway, the architectural expression of ritual transformation reached completion:

Newly arrived women occupied the most isolated and enclosed space most distant from the world of the street. Repenting Magdalens in the process of reformation occupied the middle space, and the asylum's staff lived in the building's front sections, closest to and guarding access to the world. (De Cunzo 1995: 46)

In contrast with penal institutions, such disciplinary mechanisms were incorporated into an explicitly *domestic* environment, with the spatial organization, architectural design, and living amenities—such as indoor plumbing, central heating, and a cast-iron kitchen stove—linking the asylum to the contemporary homes of Philadelphia's burgeoning nineteenth-century middle class (De Cunzo 1995: 47). Excavated ceramics suggest that rituals of liminality extended to the domestic dining table. As at other asylum sites, recovered assemblages indicate a predominance of outdated (and possibly donated) plain, edged, and transfer-printed tablewares, in addition to redware serving and eating bowls. While demonstrating a daily ritual practice of nineteenth-century dining etiquette, the Magdalen Asylum assemblage most closely resembles ceramics used by domestic servants in middle-class homes. In other words, the excavated ceramics suggest a liminal material existence poised between the specialized tablewares required for the elaborate multicourse meals of the fashionable middle class and the multipurpose single bowl characteristic of the urban poor (De Cunzo 1995: 121). While this transitional assemblage may indicate an encouragement of class aspiration and pious consumption in the asylum, the ceramics simultaneously communicate the overriding goals of institutional confinement—the ritual transformation of unmarried and sexually-active young girls into virtuous and industrious domestic servants.

But how did the Magdalens themselves experience this ritualized form of institutional confinement? Archaeological studies suggest that over the nineteenth century, asylum inmates developed a growing engagement with the institution by both actively maintaining its basic facilities and shaping its organizational directions. Early decades of operation were marked by contestations over the daily routine, with inmates petitioning the society committee in October 1830 to request increased time in the gardens for exercise and access to the fruit trees (De Cunzo 1995: 112). Asylum managers initially struggled with the frequency of escape among discontented Magdalens, although erection of a brick perimeter wall in 1842 improved compound surveillance. Most girls, however, adapted to their institutional environment, using the asylum as "a respite, though not a release from or acceptable resolution to, life's troubles" (De Cunzo 1995: 113).

By 1878, with the appointment of a new matron, the asylum rapidly transformed from a place of reformation for fallen women to a home for the improvement of wayward girls—with the institutional emphasis shifted to prevention rather than punishment. In contrast with earlier decades, these younger inmates were encouraged to actively participate in garden work as a form of regulated leisure and productive industry (De Cunzo 2001: 34–35). The asylum underwent an extended period of renewal, marked by the replacement of the old, recycled, and predominantly undecorated tablewares with the new, brightly colored, sponged and painted sets of plates, bowls, and teawares archaeologically recovered from excavated midden deposits (De Cunzo 2001: 35).

Functionally specific workrooms, classrooms, gymnasiums, courtyards, and gardens were established to support the ritualized production of healthy young working women. For the first time, the Magdalen Asylum consistently overflowed its capacity, attracting increasing numbers of young girls in search of temporary respite. Their stays decreased in length, recidivism increased, and the percentage of Magdalens released to formal employment declined dramatically as the women themselves adopted the institution as an opportune refuge, rather than as enduring salvation, from street life. This demographic pattern was linked to wider socioeconomic transitions as civic leaders of the Progressive Era managed the American workforce by shifting a growing diversity of unproductive citizens into temporary institutional forms of accommodation (De Cunzo 2001: 39; Katz 1986; also see chapter 2). In the end, decades of active engagement by asylum inmates combined with the economic demands of industrial capitalism to gradually transform this form of institutional confinement. By 1915, when the institution relocated to a larger farm outside of Philadelphia, the Magdalen Asylum served as a temporary house of education and refuge for young wayward girls as they ritually progressed toward productive adult industry.

Ultimately, a general policy emphasis on material, socioeconomic, and moral renewal had not only secularized the rehabilitative and ritualized program of the asylum, it had shifted the basic underlying aims of the American institution. In addition to providing a philanthropic mechanism for creation of an industrial workforce, institutional confinement also provided a means for neutralizing those who deviated from the social mainstream. By the Progressive Era, the asylum had become increasingly appropriated by those it incarcerated—its continuously modified built environment reflecting heterarchical or interacting modes of power rather than a simple schematic of institutional domination (see Ehrenreich et al. 1995; Wolf 1990). The Magdalen Asylum offered an actively chosen, if temporary, refuge from the rigorous demands of industrial society. But not all Americans were in a position to choose such institutional conditions. The following section will consider the material experiences of those subjected to confinement as a form of national ostracism.

Confinement as Exile

The institution was not an experience reserved exclusively for the criminal or destitute. Following the "carceral enthusiasm" of the Jacksonian era (Hirsch 1992: 66), institutional confinement emerged as a powerful mechanism for banishment in the American state. It provided for the management of those noncitizens who were deemed politically, racially, or ethnically disenfranchised from the dominant American population—undesirable groups, in other words, who previously had been simply banished beyond the national boundaries. But with consolidation of the American state over the nineteenth century, new institutional techniques were adopted to neutralize such anomalous populations *inside* the nation. Archaeology has explored places of exile through analysis of three types of institutional confinement: Civil War–era POW camps established by both the Confederate and Union armies; industrial Indian boarding schools operated by the federal government for assimilation of Native American children; and relocation camps established by the federal government for the exile of Japanese-American citizens during World War II.

Prisoner-of-War Camps and the American Civil War

Approximately 420,000 prisoners of war (POWs) endured incarceration over the four-year course of the American Civil War (Hesseltine 1930:2). By cessation of hostilities in 1865, a total of sixty-five primary facilities had been established to accommodate and neutralize captured enemy soldiers—thirty-two by the Union army and thirty-three by the Confederate army (Bush 2000: 64). These penal compounds constituted the first application of institutional management technologies to a population of people neither destitute nor criminal. As discussed in chapter 2, these sites represented the first example of mass confinement experienced by groups of Americans ambiguously identified as noncitizens because of their political affiliation.

Over the last thirty years, archaeological work has been undertaken at American Civil War POW sites associated with both sides of the conflict. Early work on the prison grounds at Andersonville National Historical Site established the location and layout of structures associated with the central penal compound (Larson and Crook 1975). By 1990, three stages of formal archaeological investigation had identified structural characteristics for the northeast corner, north gate, and southeast corner of Andersonville Prison (Prentice and Prentice 2000). Established in 1864 by the Confederate army for incarceration of captured Union soldiers, Andersonville occupied 16.5 acres of swampy land straddling both sides of Sweet Water Creek in Sumter and Macon counties of western central Georgia. Enslaved African-Americans provided labor for construction of the original penal compound. Initially designed for the accommodation of 10,000 inmates, the prison stockade was surrounded by two concentric perimeter walls constructed of locally harvested pine logs mounted upright into a 5-foot-deep (1.52 m.) wall trench and hewn square at a height of 22 feet (6.7 m.). This rectangular stockade compound encompassed an area approximately 1,010 feet (308 m.) long by 780 feet (238 m.) wide (Prentice and Prentice 2000: 169). As Union prisoners began arriving during late February 1864, an additional "deadline" of light timber fencing was erected to delineate a no-man's-land roughly 20 feet (6.1 m.) wide running along the interior of the inner perimeter wall. This additional boundary fence protected against escapes. Prisoners who entered this prohibited sector were immediately shot by Confederate guards posted at the small timber observation platforms erected along the length of the inner stockade wall at intervals of 90 feet (27.4 m.).

By June 1864, the inmate population had jumped to over 23,000 men. Confederate officials decided to extend the stockade compound northward by 610 feet (186 m.), encompassing a total area of 25 acres. In contrast with initial construction works, labor for this extension project was provided by the Union prisoners themselves. But despite this extension, overcrowding persisted, and by August 1864 the stockade confined well over 33,000 Union POWs. Historic accounts document brutal living conditions in Andersonville. Insufficient food, medicine, blankets, and clean water contributed to soaring mortality rates among the POWs. By the end of the war, a total of 12,920 deaths had been recorded by the prison hospital clerk (Bearss 1970: 147).

Archaeological excavations at Andersonville Prison exposed stockade wall trenches in both the original and extended northern sectors of the compound. Soil stratigraphy revealed significant differences in construction techniques: POWs had erected unhewn pine logs rather than the hand-hewn, squared posts set by earlier African-American slave gangs (Prentice and Prentice 2000: 177). Additionally, the uniform wall trench fills recorded in excavated sections of the original stockade contrasted sharply with the patchwork of soils backfilled around unhewn posts in the northern extension. Thus, while the perimeter fence provided a stark architecture of disciplinary segregation, differences in construction techniques may represent changes to either the organization or surveillance of two distinct yet related modes of unfree labor.

Excavations at the southeast corner of the Andersonville stockade revealed the aborted remains of a backfilled prisoner escape tunnel. Cut along the southern stockade wall, the widest section of this tunnel measured approximately 3 feet (1 m.). Since no shoring had been used during tunneling activity, several stockade posts had collapsed into the feature before it reached completion (Prentice and Prentice 2000: 185). The archaeological recovery of such blatantly subversive activities by institutional inmates provides direct material evidence of daily power negotiations in places of confinement.

A similar focus on construction methods framed archaeological research on the Confederate army POW site at Camp Ford. Established in 1863 in Smith County, East Texas, Camp Ford incarcerated a maximum of 4,800 captured Union soldiers within its compound of approximately 16 acres (Thoms 2004: 77). In contrast with Andersonville Prison, living conditions at Camp Ford were relatively humane. Adequate food rations were allocated, and freshwater was available from a stream flowing just inside the southern wall of the stockade. Archival accounts even suggest that inmates enjoyed a relatively higher living standard than those outside the stockade, with POWs negotiating the sale of their remaining cooking utensils, dishes, and tools to impoverished local citizens during end-of-war celebrations (Glover 2000).

Unlike Andersonville Prison, no preserved posts or post molds were recovered within the wall trench remains of the original Camp Ford stockade (Thoms 2004: 84). Instead, the majority of archaeological features in the study area consisted of thin sandy-clay lamellae, interpreted as surviving residues of the clay lining that sealed residential house floors. Prisoners constructed more than 1,000 dwellings within the stockade; contemporary accounts and sketches depict a "wigwam metropolis" of semisubterranean log and mud cabins packed within the perimeter walls (Thoms 2004:78). In a detailed analysis of the soil horizons from excavation trenches and a reconstruction of site formation processes, Alton Thoms links the translocation of clay throughout the site to architectural construction and site modification during the Civil War period. Confined within the heavily eroded grounds of the Camp Ford stockade, inmates endured harsh seasonal conditions that transformed the site from a cold and muddy landscape of rain-swept gullies into a desert of loose dry sand. Archaeological research indicates that POWs struggled to actively improve their adverse living conditions by importing tons of local clayey sediment "to chink hundreds of log structures, to form chimneys, mud walls, and 'sod' roofs as well as to line cabin floors" (Thoms 2004: 90). Thus, through their strategic use of a basic local soil resource, these political prisoners mobilized a form of collective everyday resistance (Scott 1990). They actively ameliorated the miserable conditions of incarceration by insulating their rough dwellings from chilly winter rains, searing summer heat, and maddening sands that blew "desperately" across the barren landscape.

Excavations at Johnson's Island Military Prison offer further insight into the

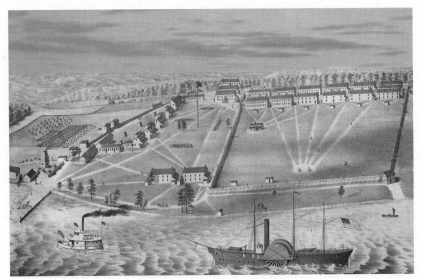

Figure 4.10. Map of Johnson's Island by Edward Gould, 1864. (Reproduced by permission of David Bush, personal collection.)

materiality of life in institutions of exile. Established in 1862 as a Union prison for Confederate officers, Johnson's Island incarcerated POWs drawn from leading Southern families—elite men who enjoyed "greater access to funds and prominent friends, both of which had the potential to make their stay more tolerable" (Bush 2000: 62). Located in Sandusky Bay of western Lake Erie (Ohio), Johnson's Island Military Prison was designed to isolate these influential captives for the duration of hostilities. Accommodation was divided into thirteen rectangular two-story blocks or communal dormitories, roughly 120 feet (36.6 m.) long by 30 feet (9.15 m.) wide. These residential blocks framed an interior parade ground (figure 4.10). Latrines were constructed to the rear of each block. The original penal compound of 14.5 acres (5.9 ha.) was expanded westwards in 1864 to alleviate overcrowding. By the end of that year, the Johnson's Island Military Prison incarcerated over 3,000 prisoners in an area of 16.5 acres (6.7 ha.). As at Andersonville Prison, a deadline of 10 feet (3 m.) ran along the interior of the stockade wall, although this feature was later expanded to 30 feet (9 m.) when the western perimeter wall was relocated.

Johnson's Island archaeological research focused on latrine features, excavating those associated with blocks 1, 6, and 8. Colloquially termed "sinks" or privies, the latrine shacks were typically 9 by 14 feet (2.7 by 4.3 m.). These structures covered unlined drop vaults with dimensions of 8 by 12 feet (2.4 by 3.7 m.) and depths ranging from 1 to 6 feet (0.3 to 1.8 m.) as dictated by the underlying bedrock (Bush 2000: 69). Used almost exclusively by the Confederate POWs, the latrines contained a variety of biological waste, secondary refuse, lost personal items, and discarded contraband materials. Recovered assemblages have been interpreted as signatures of both intentional activities and accidental discards performed by the inmates.

Drawing from both historical and sociological models (Doyle 1994; Goffman 1961), David Bush interprets three types of inmate coping strategies from the material culture of Johnson's Island Military Prison. As previously discussed in chapter 3, a typical response to the disciplinary experience of confinement involves collaboration with institutional structures, often to the point of full assimilation. At Johnson's Island, the rewards that often accompany this particular coping strategy were interpreted by Bush through comparative analysis of the glass assemblages recovered from latrines associated with different dormitory units. While block 8 housed prisoners from the general population of POWs, block 1 was used for protective custody, accommodating those Confederate officers who had elected to take the "Oath of Allegiance to the Constitution and Government of the United States" (Bush 2000: 67). Since POWs generally considered this act submissive and dishonorable, documentary records indicate that additional daily rations of bread, meat, beans, salt, and vinegar were granted as compensation. Comparison of glass assemblages revealed additional benefits that covertly accompanied the decision to collaborate. Quantities of wine, whiskey, champagne, and beer bottles were recovered from an 1864 latrine associated with block 1, with a minimum vessel count of 49 containers present. In stark contrast, a temporally comparable latrine from block 8 contained only one liquor bottle (Bush 2000: 74).

A second set of coping strategies involves prisoners' daily struggle to survive under the deprivations of institutional confinement (Sykes 1958). From the middle of 1863, as the financial and humanitarian costs of civil war climbed ever higher, the Union army sharply reduced support for POW Camps. At Johnson's Island, cuts in rations led to widespread hunger and a general lack of material goods throughout the prison. Accounts from prisoners' letters and faunal assemblages recovered from the latrines both demonstrate an increasing reliance upon supplemental food sources for basic survival, with rodent, rabbit, fish, bird, and dog consumed.

Material indicators that prisoners were trying to cope with increasingly harsh conditions are also evident in the glass assemblages. Tight cycles of abandonment and replacement enabled latrine deposits to be dated to specific years of primary use. Analysis of the glass recovered from the latrines of block 6 (the hospital unit) indicates that by 1864, medical provisions had been halved. Faced with this dramatic decrease in Union army medical supplies, the grow-

Figure 4.11. Glass bottles, Johnson's Island, Ohio. Left, U.S.A. Hospital Department pharmaceutical bottle (23.5 cm. long); right, Ayers Cherry Pectoral patent medicine bottle (18.9 cm. long). (Photographs by David Bush.)

ing population of sick and malnourished POWs mustered their own financial resources for survival. Block 6 latrines contained remains of both patent (or privately purchased) medicine vessels and pharmaceutical containers (supplied by the prison surgeon during treatments) (figure 4.11). When ratios were compared between pharmaceutical and patent bottles, the concentration of the latter rose dramatically in later 1864 latrines, even as the overall number of medicine bottles decreased. Ultimately, the ability of POWs to maintain access to restricted patent medicines reflected their elevated socioeconomic status. These captured Confederate officers were able "to buy, or buy off the surgeon" even when faced with wartime deprivations (Bush 2000: 76).

As discussed earlier in chapter 3, survival in places of confinement requires strategies for soothing the wrenching pain of emotional separation and isolation (Liebling 2000; Gallo and Ruggiero 1991; Goffman 1961). Coping methods for POWs at Johnson's Island included both letter writing and the crafting of small tokens of affection as gifts for family members outside. Latrine deposits contained quantities of hard rubber obtained and carved by the POWs into pendants, rings, pins, brooches, and crosses (Bush 2000: 74). Recovered as-

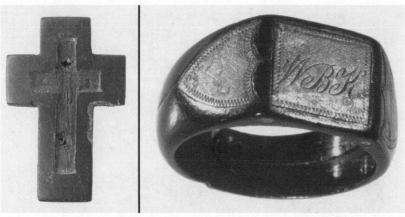

Figure 4.12. Hard rubber gutta-percha, Johnson's Island, Ohio. Left, cross made from hard rubber rule piece (2.8 cm. long); right, ring made from two buttons and three silver settings (2.4 cm. long). (Photographs by David Bush.)

semblages included off-cuts, broken attempts, and finished examples (figure 4.12). Frequently inlaid with metals, stones, and shell, these handicrafts were sometimes referred to as "gutta-percha" in inmate letters. As tokens of love, these sentimental artifacts provided POWs with not only a productive activity for relieving the monotonous boredom of confinement, but a poignant material emblem of their enduring emotional attachments to family outside the stockade walls.

Recognized by Erving Goffman (1961), a final coping mechanism adopted by inmates entails total rejection of the institutional regime. Analogous to discoveries at the Andersonville site, numerous escape tunnels located during Johnson's Island excavations attest to coordinated inmate resistance among Confederate POWs. These structures of insubordination were discovered during excavation of latrines associated with both the general population unit of block 8 and the hospital unit of block 6. Additionally, tunnels in block 8 were associated with potential escape tools: a large iron bar, a table knife, and the worn distal end of a cow long bone (Bush 2000: 71). Requiring a considerable degree of organization and subterfuge on the part of inmates, the tunnels materially represented the fermentation of collective resistance and solidarity among the prisoners.

This resistance did not go unchallenged, however. Similar to the case of the Old Rhode Island Prison, archaeologists could also read a barter of power in the institutional landscape. When Union guards grew suspicious, the penal enclosure was materially transformed in response to these stubborn escape efforts. Before the penal stockade was extended in early 1864, latrines associated with the hospital unit of block 6 were located behind the western deadline, particularly close to the stockade's western perimeter wall. Archaeological excavations of the earlier latrines revealed numerous attempts at escape tunnels dug into the back wall of the privy vaults. To thwart such activities, when the western stockade wall was extended by 95 feet (29 m.) in 1864, the deadline was expanded to 30 feet (9 m.) inside the stockade perimeter. Security was further fortified by the construction of a ditch along the interior side of these ramparts. These dramatic landscape modifications illuminate some of the dynamic power exchanges that shaped institutional life in POW camps of the American Civil War.

Thus, archaeological research has illuminated how both physical fabric and environmental landscapes were deployed in the isolation and confinement of Civil War–era enemy soldiers. These studies also demonstrated the means by which camp inmates not only minimized the discomforts and privations of their living conditions, but actively rejected their state of confinement. Assemblages of recovered materials suggest various strategies adopted by inmates to cope with the emotional, psychological, and biological pains of incarceration. Similarly, the next case studies we examine provide material evidence that ethnic and racial identity could be maintained in American institutions of exile.

The U.S. Industrial Indian Schools

Between 1875 and the mid-1930s, over 100 federal boarding schools operated across America for the accommodation and education of Native American children away from their tribal reservation lands (Adams 1995). As previously detailed in chapter 2, from 1893 the Bureau of Indian Affairs was empowered by Congress to enforce the removal and institutional enrollment of all Indian children between the ages of eight and eighteen—with threats of the reduction or removal of government rations used to induce tribal communities to relinquish their children to agency officers (Lindauer 1997: 3).

Designed to promote the vocational training and cultural assimilation of Indian students, the boarding schools adopted disciplinary institutional practices to transform Native American children into productive laborers equipped to economically participate and culturally integrate into mainstream society (Lomawaima 1994). Such philosophies of social transformation informed both the pedagogical theory and architectural designs of American schools from the mid-nineteenth century (Gibb and Beisaw 2000; Peña 1992). Thus, although operating in accordance with late Victorian educational philosophies, the U.S. Industrial Indian Schools simultaneously served as places of confinement, exile, management, and assimilation for a population identified by the state as problematic noncitizens because of their indigenous racial and cultural identities.

Established in 1891 as a large regionally based multitribal institution, the Phoenix Indian School was located on a 160-acre campus 3 miles (4.83 km) north of Phoenix, Arizona. Originally designed for 125 pupils, by 1910 the school compound had expanded to accommodate forty-eight employees, thirty-nine members of their families, and 602 Native American students. Census records demonstrate a particularly high ethnic diversity in the institution, with students enrolled from twenty-three different tribes across Arizona, New Mexico, California, Nevada, and Oregon, and school employees drawn from twenty-two different American states in addition to Mexico, Canada, Sweden, and Prussia (Trennert 1988).

Covering ten blocks, the Phoenix Indian School contained fourteen brick and twenty wood-frame buildings, including a large schoolhouse, a large six-room teaching workshop for vocational industrial trades, a two-story building providing both employee quarters and the student dining hall, several student dormitories, and a bath house. By November 1902, a boiler house generated both electricity and steam heat (Lindauer 1997: 3). The institution also encompassed fields of 240 acres surrounding the main campus, the land used primarily for vocational training in agricultural and livestock breeding.

Archaeological investigations at the Phoenix Indian School examined the remains of a large trash dump located below the southeast corner of an athletics track, a feature constructed during postwar-era modifications of the school grounds. Surface reconnaissance and test excavation trenches indicated the presence of eleven trash-filled pits containing distinct stratigraphic episodes of deposition (Barton and James 1991). Subsequent open area excavation and analysis of recovered assemblages demonstrated that the Track Site trash dated to the period between 1891 and 1926 and represented trash discarded by over 700 people—an occupational population numerically dominated by students of the institution (Lindauer 1997: 14). The artifacts therefore offer a powerful material signature of everyday life in this Native American boarding school.

Following laboratory analysis of these cultural materials, archaeologists argued that the institutional experiences of Phoenix Indian School pupils were guided by four central themes: conformity, individualism, sanitation and health, and ethnic resistance. Since institutionalization was intended to nurture the cultural assimilation of students, a large portion of the material assemblages recovered from the Track Site related to disciplinary practices of conformity and repetitive experiences of identity (De Cunzo 1995; Butler 1993; Goffman 1961).

School-issue clothing and parade uniforms, intentionally designed to echo

Figure 4.13. Ferrous metal steam whistle, Track Site, Phoenix Indian School, Arizona. (Reproduced by permission of Owen Lindauer, excavation director.)

military dress, were mandatory apparel for all students. With clothing-related artifacts representing almost 10 percent of the Track Site archaeological collection, the abundance of recovered buttons (2,164 in total) suggested a widespread adherence to institutional dress codes (Lindauer 1996: 209). While oral histories and contemporary accounts record that students discarded their traditional clothing upon enrollment, no archaeological evidence of such indigenous items was recovered from the Track Site trash dump. Instead, the button assemblage indicated a general conformity to dominant American styles of dress. A diverse range of glass, bone, shell, earthenware, rubber, and metal buttons were collected, representing specific westernized articles of clothing. This button assemblage was further linked to the imposition of patriotic and gendered identities in the institution. Shank brass buttons, for example, appeared in only two sizes: large (0.9 inch; 2.3 cm.) or small (0.59 inch; 1.5cm.). Purchased in bulk from military supply firms, these buttons were all stamp-molded with either the insignia of the U.S. Indian Service or the U.S. Army–issue bald eagle and would have decorated the parade uniforms of male students (Lindauer 1997: 21). Conversely, the small white glass, shell, and bone buttons were incorporated into western-style dresses and underclothes issued to female students.

Conformity to mainstream American gender roles was also interpreted from toys recovered from the Track Site trash dump. An MNI (minimum number of individuals) estimate of doll parts suggested that 108 porcelain dolls were represented within the ceramic assemblage, ranging in size from 6 inches (15.2 cm.) to 12 inches (30.5 cm.) tall (Lindauer and Ferguson 1996: 156). While most Indian girls would have played with handmade dolls during their earlier reservation life, these porcelain dolls were typically donated by local Phoenix businesses as Christmas gifts for the boarding school girls. Molded to resemble babies and adult ladies, the pink-and-white-colored dolls materially reflected the ethnic and gender ideologies of mainstream American society. Additionally, twenty-five miniature teacups, saucers, pitchers, and plates were discovered, suggesting a general policy of cultivating instructional role play in feminine domestic activities.

Mandatory training in vocational and domestic skills required a specific type of conformity. The replacement of environmentally experienced natural time with mechanically measured clock time was archaeologically represented by the recovery of a ferrous steam whistle from the trash dump (McKenna 1996: 164–66). Measuring 12.5 inches (32 cm.) long and 2.73 inches (7 cm.) in diameter, the steam whistle was recovered from a soil stratum dated approximately to 1912 (figure 4.13). While few students actually viewed the whistle, all school residents endured the regular blasts that dictated the start and end of activity sessions throughout each day. The whistle thus provided Native American students with a stark material introduction to the Western concept of measured time. More importantly, as an object designed to induce conformity to the repetitive regimentation of time, the steam whistle helped create an atmosphere of workplace discipline and waged labor relations within the agricultural fields and vocational training workshops of the Phoenix Indian School.

Life within this institution of exile was also shaped by the theme of individualism. In contrast with traditional tribal economies, which distributed resources on the basis of communal obligations, the competitive structures of boarding school life fostered ideas of self-reliance and individual acquisition within pupils. Since the institution aimed to promote students' cultural assimilation through their participation in the mainstream market economy, Indian students were encouraged to develop a hunger for consumer goods that could be individually earned, acquired, and enjoyed—a reward system identified as central to the broader psychological process of "institutionalization" (Sykes 1958; Goffman 1961; see chapter 3). Pupils were allowed to earn money through extra labor both on and off campus. These extra wages could then be spent on shopping expeditions in town. High frequencies of commercial beverage containers were recovered from the Track Site trash dump, suggesting that students actively supplemented their school provisions with store-bought luxuries. Carbonated soda-water bottles appeared in particularly large number throughout the site with embossments indicating that sweet beverages were particularly favored. Popular brands included Armour's Top Notch, Hires Root Beer, Hood's Sarsaparilla, and Coca-Cola, although the presence of bottled beverages such as Veronica Mineral Water and Walker's Grape Juice demon-

Figure 4.14. Bone toothbrush, Track Site, Phoenix Indian School, Arizona. Branded "The Hygienic Toothbrush" and inscribed "Lucy Miller." (Reproduced by permission of Owen Lindauer, excavation director.)

strated that the desire for commercial beverages encompassed more than fizzy drinks (Lindauer 1997: 35).

As pseudoscientific metaphors of racial difference and personal health blended seamlessly by the late nineteenth century (McClintock 1995), Indian students were taught to ensure their individual bodies were rigorously maintained as clean bodies. Pupils were instructed in both the practices and equipage necessary to achieve Western standards of personal health and hygiene. Excavations of the Track Site trash dump recovered ten plastic combs and fifty-four bone toothbrushes, objects linked to overlapping themes of individualism and health and sanitation within the Indian School environment (Lindauer 1996: 131). Contemporary accounts of boarding school life describe the daily toothbrush drills that accompanied every meal. Pupils were issued an individual toothbrush and were subsequently held responsible for its care. A variety of brands were archaeologically represented, most commonly Dr. Evans (trademark), Sanitary Ventilated, The Hygienic toothbrush, and The Sanitos—manufactured in France by E. Dupont & Co. (Lindauer 1996: 132). The numbers, names, and markings inscribed on the bone handles were probably to help students rapidly distinguish their own brush at the start of each drill (figure 4.14). Assembled in an inspection line, the pupils brushed their teeth in time to a count issued by the school matron. In this manner, three companies of twenty-two children were able to complete the toothbrush drill in only thirteen minutes. As a blatantly embodied disciplinary practice, these toothbrush drills offer a compelling example of the ritual aspects of everyday life under institutional confinement (De Cunzo 2006).

Despite this institutional regime, pupils did not passively succumb to the forces of cultural assimilation. As noted in the Track Site community report, attending an off-reservation boarding school required "a struggle between resistance and accommodation for students" (Lindauer 1997: 45). Outright insub-

Figure 4.15. Ceramic earthenware dinner plates, bifacially flaked, Phoenix Indian School, Arizona. (Reproduced by permission of Owen Lindauer, excavation director.)

ordination and absconding typically resulted in public humiliation, onerous work assignments, or corporal punishments (Trennert 1988). As a result, students adopted more subtle practices of covert noncompliance and anonymous resistance (Scott 1990) that included lighting fires, whispering conversations in native languages, smuggling foods, and sneaking off campus (Lomawaima 1994).

Archaeological work on the Track Site collections suggests that students maintained a sense of their Native American identity by curating objects and maintaining skills related to their previous lives on the tribal reservations. Since the stylistic decorations, colors, and forms of Southwestern pottery often characterized the tribal or even specific settlement origins of ceramic sherds, these excavated artifacts were interpreted as symbolic talisman, brought to the school campus by students as nostalgic material links back to their home communities. Additionally, some students expressed covert resistance by practicing traditional Native American technologies. Several handmade tools recovered from the Track Site had been fashioned by students out of institutionally available materials but worked in the same manner as chipped lithic artifacts. While most of these traditionally produced tools were manufactured from window glass or glass bottle fragments, excavations recovered several examples of white improved earthenware dinner plates with substantially flaked rims (figure

4.15). With students actively practicing and reinforcing their traditional technologies, the application of stone tool manufacture techniques was interpreted as a persistent form of cultural resistance (Lindauer 1997: 50).

Although official institutional policy imposed Christianity upon students, the practice of Native American religions flourished secretly at the Phoenix Indian School. Oral histories collected from both former students and employees indicate that students surreptitiously practiced dance ceremonies and purification rituals while enrolled (Lindauer 1997: 47). Students also brought amulets, effigies, fetishes, or charms that held religious significance along with them to the boarding school. Excavations recovered two clay miniatures, representing a bird and a four-legged animal, and a smooth nonlocal pebble sculpted into the shape of a small bone. Interpreted as possible clan totems, these spiritual objects may have been discarded in the trash dump following their discovery by boarding school staff.

Interestingly, students' shared experiences of institutional confinement resulted in the emergence of an alternative boarding school consciousness that was neither tribal nor Western. Upon her return home to the Hopi Mesa from the Phoenix Indian School in 1918, Helen Sekaquaptewa experienced a sense of profound alienation when confronted with the materiality of tribal identity:

> I didn't feel at ease in the home of my parents now. My father and mother, my sister and my older brother told me to take off those clothes and wear Hopi attire . . . I didn't wear them. . . . My mother said she was glad I was home. If I would stay there, she would not urge me to change my ways. I could wear any kind of clothes that I wanted to wear if I would just stay at home with her. (qtd. in Lindauer 1998)

Through the combined influences of educational opportunity, communal opposition to institutional authority, and shared material experiences of everyday institutional life, a powerful new sense of pan-tribal Indian identity and political consciousness was nurtured among Indian boarding school students by the early twentieth century (Lomawaima 1994; Hertzberg 1971). Thus, while the cultural assimilation of indigenous noncitizens proved futile, the experience of state-imposed institutional confinement nonetheless served as a potent, yet unintended, trajectory of cultural transformation. These fundamental issues of mainstream assimilation and evolving ethnic identity similarly frame the final case study within the category of institutional exile.

The Japanese-American Relocation Centers

Between 1942 and 1946, approximately 120,000 American men, women, and children were incarcerated within a network of assembly centers, relocation centers, and prison camps established across Arizona, Utah, Idaho, Wyoming, Colorado, Arkansas, and inland regions of California (Daniels et al. 1991). Eerily echoing the Indian boarding schools only a decade earlier, this twentieth-century population of Americans was subjected to years of federally imposed institutional confinement solely on the basis of racial and ethnic identity. By the 1980s, the U.S. federal commission established to reassess the relocation policies of the Roosevelt administration officially determined that factors of wartime hysteria, failed civic leadership, and racial prejudice had all contributed to the treatment of Japanese-Americans during World War II. Nonetheless, the enduring material legacy of this shameful episode of institutional confinement illuminates profound underlying questions of both citizenship and civil rights.

Since the mid-1990s, a series of archaeological research projects and commemoration programs have been undertaken to explore the cultural heritage of these World War II–era Japanese-American relocation sites. Both community outreach and project publications have generated strong emotional responses from former internees and their descendants. These reactions have focused public attention on the ambiguous relationship between the American state and its multicultural society—particularly as some former internees had long concealed their confinement experiences from descendants to avoid perpetuating resentment of the American government (Farrell and Burton 2004: 24).

The first relocation center to undergo sustained archaeological study was the Manzanar National Historic Site in eastern California (Burton 1996), although more recent work has expanded to include a detailed inventory of archival and archaeological resources from all relocation centers (Burton et al. 1999). Additionally, the U.S. National Park Service established archaeological recording and assessment projects at the Minidoka Internment National Monument (Idaho), the Heart Mountain Relocation Center (Wyoming), the Topaz Relocation Center (Utah), the Tule Lake Segregation Center (California), and the Catalina Honor Camp, a former prison camp in the Coronado National Forest (Arizona) associated with the incarceration of Japanese-American and other draft resisters during World War II (Farrell and Burton 2004; Burton and Farrell 2001). Like other places of institutional exile, the Japanese-American relocation centers hold primary significance for their negative impact on the ethnic community's traditions, social structure, and financial security.

Initial results of archaeological research demonstrated patterns in the design, layout, and provision of the relocation centers. As previously outlined in chapter 2, the sites were established and administered by the federal War Relocation Authority to operate as self-contained fortified compounds. At the thirteen primary relocation centers, surface feature inventories documented substantial remains of a standardized set of structures and facilities—including administration quarters, warehouses and factories, hospitals, barracks, fire stations, and high schools (Burton et al. 1999: 6). Site surveys also recorded the frequent survival of security-related features (perimeter fences, watchtowers, sentry posts) and outlying auxiliary support facilities (cemeteries, irrigation canals, water tanks and reservoirs, pumping plants, and sewage disposal machinery). Various features recorded at the relocation centers represent official policies of minimizing operational costs. To contribute toward the war effort, a number of factories were established at Manzanar. In July 1942, Roy Nash, first director of this relocation center, proudly described its camouflage net factory to journalists:

> Five hundred American citizens stand daily in great sheds, weaving burlap patterns into nets which hang from a 20-foot ceiling, patterns for summer, patterns for winter, patterns for the desert. . . . Five hundred nets a day go out from Manzanar. Boys and girls mostly in their early twenties work . . . with masks over their mouths against the dust. They work for the prize of a watermelon for the crew that puts out the most. . . . They work perfectly aware that they are contributing to America's war effort, and all they ask is that their fellow citizens may hear, and some day understand. (Nash 1996: 111)

Facilities for livestock and farming were established throughout the relocation centers, with archaeological evidence suggesting the Minidoka center additionally supported a motor pool and extensive tin can recycling (Burton and Farrell 2001; Burton et al. 1999). In addition, rubbish landfills were located and recorded at six relocation centers, their accumulated contents providing valuable material perspectives on the nature of both official federal provisions and treasured personal possessions in the encampments.

Results of archaeological research at the internment camps offer new perspectives on not only the mundane embodied experience of twentieth-century institutional life, but also the strategic means by which internees maintained a sense of ethnic identity under the austere regulations of confinement. While the oral histories of some local Anglo-Americans residents minimize the degree of confinement associated with the relocation centers (Farrell and Burton 2004: 22), both site inventories and archaeological surveys confirm that the sites were run as fortified places of incarceration. Concrete footings and foundations of security watchtowers were recorded at both the Manzanar and Tule Lake relocation centers, with similar features inventoried at the Granada, Jerome, and Topaz centers. At the Manzanar site, archival blueprints indicate that eight watchtowers provided surveillance from the corners and midsections of the fenced central compound. Remains of the seven relocated watchtowers typically consist of four 18-inch (46-cm.) square steel and concrete footing blocks (or posts) arranged into a square of 11 feet (3.4 m.) and thus providing a structural foundation for the elevated surveillance platform (Burton 1996: 300).

During the 2002 excavation season at the Minidoka Internment National Monument, project participants cleared and recorded basalt and mortar stone structures at the entrance gate housing the original reception building and military police compound (Burton et al. 2003). Other surviving fortification systems remnants include architectural elements of sentry stations and barbed wire perimeter fences at the Granada, Heart Mountain, Manzanar, Rohwer, Topaz, and Tule Lake relocation centers. Thus, both architectural and landscape features provide an enduring archaeological testimony to the conditions of confinement, segregation, domination, and surveillance that characterized daily life in these institutions of exile (Markus 1995).

The second theme to emerge from archaeological research at the internment sites involves the maintenance of ethnic identity in these stark institutional settings. Although the War Relocation Authority provided standardized accommodation and portable living resources for all relocation centers (see table 2.3), archaeological research suggests that evacuees personalized their institutional world. Artifactual assemblages and landscape features indicate both the persistence of Japanese culture and its rich fusion with mainstream American culture, even while such non-normative expressions of identity risked sanctions (Farrell and Burton 2004). Thus, these archaeological sites illuminate not only the hidden transcripts of collective resistance (Scott 1990), but the personal coping strategies and inmate solidarity practices that often flourish in places of confinement (see Goffman 1961; Gallo and Ruggiero 1991; Sykes and Messinger 1960).

Despite restricted luggage allowances, many internees brought family heirlooms and nostalgic objects with them when evacuated from their coastal homes. The primary rubbish landfill associated with the Minidoka relocation center was identified on public land administered by the Bureau of Land Management, one mile north of the national monument. Consisting of a large, partially filled pit approximately 370 feet by 100 feet (113 m. by 31 m.), the refuse feature contained abundant remains of metal garbage cans, structural furnishings, and domestic artifacts associated with the relocation center (Burton and Farrell 2001: 97). Amid the institutional debris of generic white American "hotelwares" (Burton 1996: 807), a remarkably high presence of Japanese domestic ceramics (particularly blue-on-white and polychrome porcelain bowls) and Asian glass candy containers were recorded in surface deposits. Similar assemblages were recovered from the central, barrack, and hospital landfill middens excavated at the Manzanar relocation center (figure 4.16). These central compound deposits also contained traditional Japanese porcelain teacups, sake cups, serving plates, ornamental figurines, and stoneware bowls in addition to nine tokens from the classic Asian strategy game *Go*, manufactured from polished stones in both black and white variants (Burton 1996: 806, 880).

Figure 4.16. Ceramics, Manzanar Relocation Center, California. (Reproduced by permission of Jeffery F. Burton, Western Archaeological and Conservation Center, National Park Service.)

Figure 4.17. Cemetery monument, Manzanar Relocation Center, California. (Reproduced by permission of Jeffery F. Burton, Western Archaeological and Conservation Center, National Park Service.)

By indicating "that Japanese American internees made considerable efforts to maintain traditional foodways" despite the provision of communal meals at the mess hall block, these ceramic assemblages suggest an enduring material continuity of Japanese-American identity within these austere institutional environments (Majewski 1996: 809).

Expressions of ethnicity also infused landscape features constructed by the internees at many of the relocation centers. Five relocation centers retained substantial remains of cemeteries, with standing monuments or headstones recorded at Granada, Manzanar, and Rohwer. At the Manzanar cemetery, internees erected and inscribed a concrete commemorative obelisk in Japanese: the front or east-face inscription translates as "Monument to console the souls of the dead" and the rear or west-face inscription translates as "Erected by the Manzanar Japanese August 1943" (Burton et al. 2001: 9). A concrete slab and nine concrete posts, shaped and stained to resemble wood, completed the funerary monument (figure 4.17). The Rohwer cemetery contains twenty-four standardized cast concrete headstones and two concrete markers, all constructed by evacuees to face toward the relocation center. Crafted in the shape of a military tank, the first monument was erected to commemorate Japanese-American troops of the combined 100th Battalion and 442nd

Regimental Combat Team killed during Italian and French campaigns. The second, commemorating those who had died while incarcerated in Rohwer, was inscribed in Japanese and translates as "May the people of Arkansas keep in beauty and reverence forever this ground where our bodies sleep" (Burton et al. 1999: 256).

The design of rock alignments, gardens, and ponds built within the camps' civilian zones typically reflect traditional Japanese concepts of order, beauty, and harmony. According to archaeological surveys and historic photographs, many of the residential blocks at Manzanar were ornamented with large community ponds and garden complexes. Similarly, the most significant remains of the hospital compound consisted of an elaborate pond and garden complex on the eastern side of the doctors' quarters, rock alignments along the eastern road, rock circles around trees, and rock sculptures around the hospital administration building region (Burton et al. 1999: 179). At Minidoka, archaeological work conducted during the summer of 2001 identified features related to the ornamental entrance garden. Installed in June 1944 by a team of evacuees, the tree-lined garden was designed by chief gardener Fujitaro Kubota in a fusion of traditional symbolic Japanese landscape principles and American aesthetics of wartime modernism. While no photographs or plans exist to document the

Figure 4.18. Japanese inscription at the setting basin translated "Beat Great Britain and the USA," Manzanar Relocation Center, California. (Reproduced by permission of Jeffery F. Burton, Western Archaeological and Conservation Center, National Park Service.)

garden layout, archaeological survey recorded two large earthen mounds with symbolic basalt rock sculptures, two low rock-covered mounds, two possible pathways, and stepping stones, all enclosed within a ring of trees (Burton et al. 2003: 10). Intended to ornament both the fortified entrance gate and the honor roll monument that listed the names of Japanese-American servicemen from Minidoka, the garden served to communicate a merging of American patriotism and Japanese traditions. As material expressions of shared ethnic affiliation and collective labor, the decorative landscape features recorded at many of the relocation centers also provide an eloquent statement of evacuee solidarity—of a new social cohesion explicitly nurtured through the communal experience of institutional confinement (Farrell and Burton 2004; see chapter 3 for a broader discussion of inmate subcultures under incarceration).

Some expressions of internee solidarity evince a more resistant tone. At the Manzanar Relocation Center, over 175 inscriptions were recorded, including over forty dates and fifty different names written into the wet concrete of construction works undertaken by evacuees (Inomata and Burton 1996) (figure 4.18). While the majority of these inscriptions appear to communicate pride or recognition of workmanship, others suggest resentment or defiance. A Japanese poem, or tanka, was inscribed by an anonymous author into a concrete pipeline support in the south fields irrigation system (Inomata and Burton 1996: 664). Written in Chinese characters (figure 4.19, right), the inscription translates:

> Pleasantly we will soon reap all spikes
> If you want to be proud, be proud for now
> Ugly rice (Americans?)

Carrying a double meaning, the poem simultaneously celebrates the harvesting of rice and triumph over the American forces. The final two characters (*shu-hi*) have also been translated as "ugly despicable people."

In some cases, evacuee graffiti was explicitly militaristic. Among the Manzanar inscriptions, the Japanese military government motto *chukun aikoku* (figure 4.19, upper left)—"Loyal to the Emperor and Love the Country"—appeared in Japanese characters on the wall of a concrete water supply reservoir (Inomata and Burton 1996: 663). The slogans "Banzai, The Great Japanese Empire, Manzanar Black Dragon Group Headquarters" and simply "Banzai Nippon" (figure: 4.19, lower left) were etched into other concrete elements of the compound's water supply system (Burton et al. 1999: 194–97).

Heritage inventories at Tule Lake Segregation Center, a special high-security facility in Northern California, recorded a particularly high frequency of graffiti authored by Japanese-American prisoners. Established to isolate the hundreds

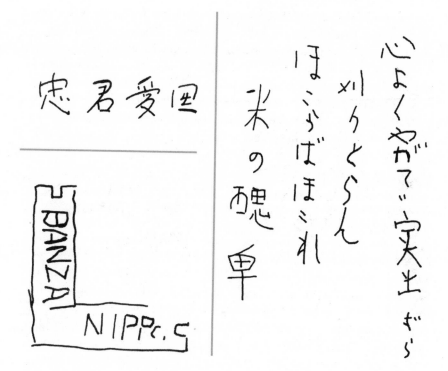

Figure 4.19. Anonymous graffiti transcriptions, Manzanar Relocation Center, California. (Reproduced by permission of Jeffery F. Burton, Western Archaeological and Conservation Center, National Park Service.)

of evacuees considered disloyals or troublemakers, the stockade cell block contained thousands of messages. Drawings included insects, flowers, and a Japanese flag. Japanese inscriptions ranged from stubborn protests, such as "Today was wrongfully accused of disorder problem" and "The Great Japanese Empire," to melancholic and poetic reflections, including (in English) "When the golden sun has sunk beyound [*sic*] the desert horizon and darkness followed, under a dim light casting my lonesome heart" and the simple poignant plea, "Show me the way to go to home" (Burton and Farrell 2005: 9, 11).

Today, these recent historic monuments to the American experience of institutional confinement serve a dual role. The relocation centers provide places of both collective and personal commemoration for former internees and their families. The Manzanar Cemetery serves as a particular focus for ceremonial events, with the Manzanar Pilgrimage held annually on the last Saturday in April. In addition to this large public gathering at the central obelisk shrine, smaller personal and family commemorations occur in the form of artifacts and mementos placed on both the cemetery monument and graves by site visitors throughout the year (Burton et al. 2001: 11). Secondly, as twentieth-century places of involuntary exile, the Japanese-American relocation centers provide a testimony to the painful institutional experiences endured by a category of Americans identified solely on the basis of their ethnic affiliation. Through programs of research and public outreach, these sites encourage the development of broader public debate over civil rights, citizenship, and the role of institutional confinement in modern American society.

Conclusions

Places of institutional confinement retain a profound materiality—a system of material meanings clearly accessible to archaeological research. From the protoindustrial craft production of shell wampum in the late seventeenth-century Albany Almshouse, through the early nineteenth-century assembly-line production of the congregate-system Old Rhode Island Penitentiary, to the war-effort factories of the twentieth-century Japanese-American relocation centers, concerns over the nature and organization of unfree labor have plagued the American institution. Despite the optimistic intentions of the New Republic, archaeological perspectives on historic American prisons and asylums suggest that these places offered an ambiguous mix of living standards and disciplinary work regimes. Although some sites may have utilized concepts of "the domestic" to accommodate or ritually transform their involuntary occupants, the artifacts, physical fabric, and cultural landscapes of other American institutions can be read as a reciprocal materiality of harsh discipline and stubborn insubordination.

Following the Civil War, as African-American men began to constitute an increasing component of the incarcerated population and Native American communities fell under the voracious grasp of the expansionist state, difficult questions of labor and living conditions immediately raised broader ethical debates over citizenship and civil rights. For whom was the American state responsible? How could anomalous members of the population be safely accommodated, neutralized, and rehabilitated? How could privatization be adopted to ameliorate the rising expense of institutional management? What material conditions would constitute minimum standards?

Finally, profound issues of social solidarity, personal dignity, and everyday resistance infused the materiality of institutional confinement. As inmates used material culture to express their social identities, they actively forged enduring ethnic and emotive links to each other and to the world outside the perimeter walls. By making creative use of surrounding resources to cope with the austerity, deprivation, and humiliations of the institutional regime, inmates collectively and individually produced their own alternative material records. Archaeological explorations of the American institution offer a testimony to their enduring spirit of survival.

5

Privations

A Materiality of Institutional Confinement

For prison life with its endless privations and restrictions makes one rebellious. The most terrible thing about it is not that it breaks one's heart—hearts are made to be broken—but that it turns one's heart to stone. . . . And he who is in a state of rebellion cannot receive grace . . . for in life as in art the mood of rebellion closes up the channels of the soul, and shuts out the airs of heaven.

—Oscar Wilde, *De profundis*

The American experience of institutional confinement is essentially a story of power and endurance. This volume has examined various historical, theoretical, and archaeological perspectives to consider the nature, purpose, and role of confinement as a particularly modern phenomenon. But despite four centuries of theoretical and historical evolution—including growing sophistication in the diverse applications and embodiments of its force—we are still left to contemplate an underlying purpose. What is achieved by the institutional experience?

For many advocates, practitioners, and professionals in the fields of criminal justice, corrective services, and clinical psychiatry, institutional life offers the promise of rehabilitation for those who do not (or cannot) function as self-sustaining, productive, or law-abiding citizens. It provides a necessary external structure for those prisoners, patients, inmates, or clients who require custodial care. Thus, the American institution can be seen as a place of "supervised liberty" (Pratt 2002)—a site for detoxification, for medical treatment, for obtaining reliable food and a dry bed, for improving literacy and achieving educational certificates, for learning anger management and industrial skills (see Tonry and Petersilia 2000; N. Morris 1998).

But does confinement itself create delinquency? As the first-timer becomes habituated to the disciplinary regime and assimilated into inmate subcultures, does the asylum or prison itself fabricate a dependent recidivist? Many scholars argue that institutional life also operates as a form of population warehousing. From the mid-1990s, inmates of federal institutions have been overwhelmingly denied access to higher education. As a result of the federal Work Opportunity and Personal Responsibility Act of 1996, former prisoners, even following successful completion of their parole period, remain excluded from public aid programs, including Medicaid, public housing, veterans' benefits, and food stamps. Since all but four states deny those in detention facilities the right to vote, institutional inmates are restricted from political participation. Given disproportionate rates of incarceration by race in contemporary America, one out of every seven African-American adult men is denied full rights of citizenship (Wacquant 2001: 106). Serving to sustain an exclusionary relationship between the American state and its citizenry, institutional confinement can therefore be judged as a painful form of civic death.

What can archaeology add to these contrasting portraits of penal form and function? Four distinct themes have emerged from the case studies in this book. First, over the last four centuries, places of confinement have provided a diverse range of living conditions. Establishments such as the Old Baton Rouge Penitentiary, Uxbridge Almshouse, Cook County Poor Farm, and the Andersonville POW Camp were typically characterized by material deprivation, surveillance, overcrowding, physical punishment, sickness, injury, and death. Archaeological work on other institutions, such as the Walnut Street Prison, Alcatraz Island, the Phoenix Indian School, and even the Manzanar and Minidoka relocation centers, indicate that adequate (if frugal, monotonous, and heavily regulated) material resources characterized institutional life. Some charitable institutions, such as the New York City Almshouse, Falmouth Poor House, and Magdalen Asylum, even appear to have cultivated a humane environment of purposeful domesticity, supporting children's play activities and permitting personal possessions within their walls. But despite such variations, these places of confinement were all fabricated for the care, punishment, and reform of people outside the mainstream of American society.

Further, such regulated accommodation was inevitably supported by institutionally managed forms of unfree labor. Modes of labor ranged from industrial production in the congregate workshops of the Old Rhode Island Penitentiary and the camouflage net factory of the Manzanar relocation camp, to craft production in the wampum shell activity areas of the Albany Almshouse. Unfree labor was typically gendered, with females trained in textile manufacture, domestic services, and housekeeping duties, while male inmates worked on either outdoor agricultural projects or industrial production in institutional workshops. Male inmates frequently provided labor for the construction and maintenance of the institutions that housed them, as demonstrated in structural and stratigraphic evidence from not only nineteenth-century penitentiaries and Civil War POW camps but also the Japanese-American relocation camps of World War II. Detailed archaeological analysis of these construction projects has further established the landscape of confinement as a built environment of ethnic expression, of insubordinate work practices, and of enduring self-expression.

Third, archaeology offers fresh understandings of the materiality of institutional confinement. Theoretical investigations of incarceration depict the experience of institutional life as a strenuous and perpetual expression of power—both the power of the asylum to transform its occupants and the power of those inmates to cope within this arduous environment. Archaeological research illuminates how the physical fabric of institutional architecture itself demonstrates power—how the stone perimeter walls of the Walnut Street Prison, the "dark cells" of the Old Rhode Island Prison, the doorways and halls of the Magdalen Asylum, the restricted deadline of the Andersonville POW camp, and the sentry posts and barbed wire fences of the Manzanar relocation center all performed a specific coercive and corporeal role in the institutional landscape.

Detailed analysis of excavated materials similarly demonstrates how the provision of obsolete ceramics, frugal room furnishings, standardized uniforms, limited medical supplies, and mandatory equipment for hygiene drills helped to cultivate a docile consciousness among confined individuals. Archaeological perspectives emphasize the intrinsic materiality of coping, negotiation, resistance, and survival in American institutions. By recording and interpreting evidence of resistance—the alcohol bottles and bone dice of the Old Baton Rouge Penitentiary; the modified spoon-handle skeleton key of Alcatraz Island; the porcelain figurine fragment of the Falmouth Poor House; the escape tunnels and gutta-percha crafts of the Johnson's Island POW camp; the traditionally flaked ceramic plates and tribal amulets of the Phoenix Indian School trash pit; the Asian ceramic assemblages and inmate graffiti of the Minidoka and Manzanar relocation centers—archaeology gives radical new voice to the hidden transcripts of institutional confinement (Scott 1990).

Finally, by exploring the constitutive material conditions of institutional confinement, archaeological case studies can illuminate temporal patterns in the accommodation and treatment of those on the margins of society. On one hand, the American institution has evolved dramatically since its origins in the colonial era. Living conditions have been modernized. Legislators, activists, administrators, and legal advocates have established minimum levels of provision and basic standards for humane care under confinement. Over the last five decades, a decreasing diversity of institutional types has reshaped the nature of confinement, as disenfranchised groups were no longer routinely accommodated the in grand asylums, workhouses, and industrial schools of the nineteenth century. By the late twentieth century, one specific form of confinement—the prison—has not only dominated, but exemplified, the American institutional experience.

Nonetheless, with the advent of mass incarceration, penal confinement has itself evolved to encompass the same multiple functions and diverse populations previously served by those different types of institutions. American penal facilities range from low-security compounds characterized by shared residential dormitory accommodation to super-maximum high-tech penitentiaries designed for the stark isolation of exceptional inmates. There are "open prisons" virtually indistinguishable from farms; there are "prisons with tennis courts and prisons where the only out-of-cell exercise is an hour of pacing an outdoor cage three times a week" (N. Morris 1998: 202).

In terms of inmate crime statistics, by the end of the twentieth century, approximately 63 percent of federal prisoners had been convicted for drug offenses, 15 percent for violent crimes, and only 7 percent for property offenses (Department of Justice 1999: 3). Population expansion rates have been the highest among female inmates, with extortion (13 percent) and drug offenses (67 percent) constituting the bulk of female convictions by 1995 (Fleisher 2001: 685). Most American penal facilities offer specialized support—including vocational training, education programs, health care, religious services, and treatment programs for mental illness, disabilities, and substance abuse (N. Morris 1998). A patchwork of administrative systems exists across federal, state, and hybrid jurisdictions to accommodate the needs of this increasingly diverse inmate population. Is the twenty-first-century prison—this ubiquitous form of American institutional confinement—all that different from the generic multifunctional institutions of the seventeenth century?

Institutional confinement remains a constant, if not expanding, element of American life. Inevitably, by revealing both transformations and continuities in the nature of the institution over the past three centuries, archaeology has returned to the profound question of purpose. Why confine people within an institution? Does the material experience of incarceration rehabilitate the inmate? Does it protect American society from those who are dangerous, dependent, or merely different? By interrogating the temporal and situational nature of this delicate balance between civic protection and human rights, the case studies in this volume have explored the underlying constitution and integrity of American society itself.

The archaeology of institutional confinement offers a compelling material perspective on this confronting aspect of the American experience. It reveals the moral anxieties and civic ambiguities that immediately arise when we question how to best accommodate those who do not, or cannot, participate in mainstream society. By recording the material nature of these austere monuments, archaeology ensures we acknowledge and reflect upon the enduring legacy of the American institution as we enter the twenty-first century.

References

Adams, D. W. 1995. *Education for Extinction: American Indians and the Boarding School Experience 1875–1928.* Lawrence: University of Kansas Press.

Addams, J. 1910. *Twenty Years at Hull House.* New York: Macmillan.

Althusser, L. 1971. "Ideology and Ideological State Apparatuses." In *Lenin and Philosophy and Other Essays*, edited by L. Althusser, 121–73. London: New Left Books.

———. 1984. *Essays on Ideology.* London: Verso.

Amnesty International. 2005a. "Guantánamo—An Icon of Lawlessness." January 6. http://www.web.amnesty.org/library/index/ENGAMR510022005 (accessed February 20, 2007).

Amnesty International. 2005b. "Guantánamo Bay—A Human Rights Scandal." http://www.web.amnesty.org/pages/guantanamobay-background-eng (accessed February 20, 2007).

Atwood, M. 1996. *Alias Grace.* London: Bloomsbury Publishing.

Bakhtin, M. M. 1981. *The Dialogic Imagination: Four Essays.* Austin: University of Texas Press.

Barton, C. M., and S. R. James. 1991. *The Phoenix Indian School Archaeological Project: Results of the Test Excavations.* Anthropological Field Studies 25. Tempe: Arizona State University, Office of Cultural Resource Management.

Baugher, S. 2001. "Visible Charity: The Archaeology, Material Culture, and Landscape Design of New York City's Municipal Almshouse Complex, 1736–1797." *International Journal of Historical Archaeology* 5(2): 175–202.

Baugher, S., and E. J. Lenik 1997. "Anatomy of an Almshouse Complex." *Northeast Historical Archaeology* 26: 1–22.

BBC. 2002. "Profile: Jose Padilla." http://news.bbc.co.uk/1/hi/world/americas/2037444.stm (accessed February 20, 2007).

———. 2005a. "Documents Show Guantánamo Claims." http://news.bbc.co.uk/1/hi/uk/4217707.stm (accessed February 20, 2007).

———. 2005b. "Guantánamo Bosnians Cry 'Torture.'" http://news.bbc.co.uk/1/hi/world/americas/4443449.stm (accessed February 20, 2007).

———. 2005c. "Guantánamo Hunger Strikers Double." http://news.bbc.co.uk/1/hi/world/americas/4568152.stm (accessed February 20, 2007).

———. 2006. "Guantánamo Bay Inmates 'Tortured.'" http://news.bbc.co.uk/1/hi/world/americas/4710966.stm (accessed February 20, 2007).

Bearss, E. C. 1970. *Andersonville National Historic Site: Historic Resource Study and Historic Base Map.* Washington, D.C.: National Park Service, U.S. Department of the Interior.

Beaudry, M. C., L. Cook, and S. Mrozowski. 1991. "Artifacts and Active Voices: Material

Culture as Social Discourse." In *The Archaeology of Inequality*, edited by R. McGuire and R. Paynter, 150–91. Oxford: Basil Blackwell.

Beaumont, G. de, and A. de Tocqueville. 1965 [1833]. *On the Penitentiary System in the United States and its Application in France*. Carbondale: Southern Illinois University Press.

Becker, R. J., and M. S. Nassaney. 2005. "An Archaeological Assessment of the Asylum Lake/Colony Farm Orchard Property in Kalamazoo, Michigan." Report of Investigations No. 109. Kalamazoo: Department of Anthropology, Western Michigan University. http://www.wmich.edu/asylumlake/social/Social%20History%20Index%20Page.htm (accessed August 15, 2006).

Bell, C. 1992. *Ritual Theory, Ritual Practice*. New York: Oxford University Press.

Bentham, J. 1791. *Panopticon; or the Inspection House*. Dublin: Tomas Byrne.

Berridge, C. 1987. *The Almshouses of London*. Southampton: Ashford Press.

Bourdieu, P. 1977. *Outline of a Theory of Practice*. Cambridge: Cambridge University Press.

———. 1998. *Practical Reason*. Cambridge: Polity Press.

Bowker, L. H. 1981. "Gender Differences in Prisoner Subcultures." In *Women and Crime in America*, edited by L. H. Bowker, 409–19. New York: Macmillan.

Bowler, A. E. 1997. "Asylum Art: The Social Construction of an Aesthetic Category." In *Outsider Art*, edited by V. Zolberg and J. Cherbo, 11–36. Cambridge: Cambridge University Press.

Box, S. 1987. *Recession, Crime and Unemployment*. London: Macmillan.

Braverman, H. 1974. *Labor and Monopoly Capital*. New York: Monthly Review Press.

Bright, C. 1996. *The Powers that Punish*. Ann Arbor: University of Michigan Press.

Brockway, Z. R. 1910. "The American Reformatory Prison System." In *Prison Reform: Correction and Prevention*, edited by Z. R. Brockway, 88–107. New York: Russell Sage Foundation.

Brodie, A., J. Croom, and J. O. Davies. 2002. *English Prisons: An Architectural History*. Swindon: English Heritage.

Brown, E. A. 1952. *Stubborn Fool: A Narrative*. Cadwell, Idaho: Caxton Printers.

Burton, J. F. 1996. *Three Farewells to Manzanar: The Archeology of Manzanar National Historic Site, California*. Western Archeological and Conservation Center Publications in Anthropology 67. Tucson: National Park Service.

Burton, J. F., L. S. Bergstresser, and A. H. Tamura. 2003. *Minidoka Internment National Monument: Archaeology at the Gate*. Western Archaeological and Conservation Center. Tucson: National Park Service.

Burton, J. F., and M. M. Farrell. 2001. *This Is Minidoka: An Archeological Survey of Minidoka Internment National Monument, Idaho*. Western Archeological and Conservation Center Publications in Anthropology 80. Tucson: National Park Service.

———. 2005. "Tule Lake Segregation Center." Unpublished National Historic Landmark Nomination. Western Archaeological and Conservation Center. Tucson: National Park Service.

Burton, J. F., M. M. Farrell, F. B. Lord, and R. W. Lord. 1999. *Confinement and Ethnicity:*

An Overview of World War II Japanese American Relocation Sites. Western Archeological and Conservation Center Publications in Anthropology 74. Tucson: National Park Service.

Burton, J. F., J. D. Haines, and M. M. Farrell. 2001. *I Rei To: Archeological Investigations at the Manzanar Relocation Center Cemetery, Manzanar National Historic Site, California.* Western Archeological and Conservation Center Publications in Anthropology 79. Tucson: National Park Service.

Bush, D. 2000. "Interpreting the Latrines of the Johnson's Island Civil War Military Prison." *Historical Archaeology* 34(1): 62–78.

Butler, J. 1993. *Bodies That Matter: On the Discursive Limits of "Sex."* London: Routledge.

———. 1997. *The Psychic Life of Power: Theories in Subjection.* Stanford: Stanford University Press.

Butler, J., and J. Scott. 1992. *Feminists Theorize the Political.* New York: Routledge.

Carlen, P. 1983. *Women's Imprisonment: A Study in Social Control.* London: Routledge.

———. 1998. *Sledgehammer: Women's Imprisonment at the Millennium.* London: MacMillan.

Carleton, M. T. 1971. *Politics and Punishment: The History of the Louisiana State Penal System.* Baton Rouge: Louisiana State University Press.

Carroll, L. 1997. "Hacks, Blacks, and Cons: Race Relations in a Maximum-Security Prison." In Marquart and Sorensen, *Correctional Contexts*, 140–57.

Casella, E. C. 2000. "'Doing Trade': A Sexual Economy of Nineteenth-century Australian Convict Prisons." *World Archaeology* 32(2): 209–21.

———. 2001. "Landscapes of Punishment and Resistance: A Female Convict Settlement in Tasmania, Australia." In *Contested Landscapes: Movement, Exile and Place*, edited by B. Bender and M. Winer, 103–20. Oxford: Berg.

———. 2002. *Archaeology of the Ross Female Factory: Female Incarceration in Van Diemen's Land, Australia.* Records of the Queen Victoria Museum, No. 108. Launceston: Queen Victoria Museum and Art Gallery.

Christianson, S. 1998. *With Liberty for Some: 500 Years of Imprisonment in America.* Boston: Northeastern University Press.

Clemmer, D. R. 1940. *The Prison Community.* Boston: Christopher Publishing House.

Cohen, E. A. 1954. *Human Behaviour in the Concentration Camp.* London: Jonathan Cape.

Collins, C. 1998. "Through the Lens of Assimilation: Edwin L. Chalcraft and Chemawa Indian School." *Oregon Historical Quarterly* 98(14): 390–425.

Comaroff, J., and J. Comaroff. 1991. *Of Revelation and Revolution.* Vol. 1, *Christianity, Colonialism, and Consciousness in South Africa.* Chicago: Chicago University Press.

Conover, T. 2000. *Newjack: Guarding Sing Sing.* New York: Random House.

Cook, L. J. 1991. "The Uxbridge Poor Farm in the Documentary Record." In Elia and Wesolowsky, *Archaeological Excavations*, 40–81.

Cotter, J. L., R. W. Moss, B. C. Gill, and J. Kim. 1988. *The Walnut Street Prison Workshop.* Philadelphia: Athenæum of Philadelphia.

Crumley, C. L. 1987. "A Dialectical Critique of Hierarchy." In *Power Relations and State Formation*, edited by T. C. Patterson and C. W. Gailey, 155–69. Washington, D.C.: American Anthropological Association.

Damousi, J. 1997. *Depraved and Disorderly: Female Convicts, Sexuality and Gender in Colonial Australia*. Cambridge: Cambridge University Press.

Daniels, R., S. C. Taylor, and H. H. L. Kitano. 1991. *Japanese Americans from Relocation to Redress*. Rev. ed. Seattle: University of Washington Press.

Davis, A. F. 1967. *Spearheads for Reform: The Social Settlements and the Progressive Movement 1890–1914*. New York: Oxford University Press.

De Cunzo, L. A. 1995. "Reform, Respite, Ritual: An Archaeology of Institutions: the Magdalen Society of Philadelphia, 1800–1850." *Historical Archaeology* 29(3): 1–168.

———. 2001. "On Reforming the 'Fallen' and Beyond: Transforming Continuity at the Magdalen Society of Philadelphia, 1845–1916." *International Journal of Historical Archaeology* 5(1): 19–43.

———. 2006. "Exploring the Institution: Reform, Confinement, Social Change." In *Historical Archaeology*, edited by M. Hall and S. W. Silliman, 167–89. Oxford: Blackwell.

Delgado, J. P. 1991. *Alcatraz: Island of Change*. San Francisco: Golden Gate National Park Association.

Dennis, D. 1995. "Death of the Big Yard." In Foster, Rideau, and Dennis, *The Wall is Strong*, 301–6.

Department of Justice. 1999. *Substance Abuse and Treatment, State and Federal Prisoners, 1997*. Special Report NCJ-172871. Washington, D.C.: Bureau of Justice Statistics.

DeWitt, J. 1943 *Final Report, Japanese Evacuation from the West Coast, 1942*. Washington, D.C.: U.S. Government Printing Office.

Dix, D. L. 1843. "Memorial to the Legislature of Massachusetts." Boston: Munroe & Francis.

———. 1845. *Remarks on Prisons and Prison Discipline in the United States*. 2nd ed. Philadelphia: Kite.

Dobash, R. P., R. E. Dobash, and S. Gutteridge. 1986. *The Imprisonment of Women*. Oxford: Basil Blackwell.

Douglas, M. 1966. *Purity and Danger*. New York: Praeger.

Doyle, R. 1994. *Voices from Captivity: Interpreting the American POW Narrative*. Lawrence: University Press of Kansas.

Driver, F. 1993. *Power and Pauperism: The Workhouse System, 1834–1884*. Cambridge: Cambridge University Press.

Durkheim, E. 1964. *The Division of Labor in Society* New York: Free Press.

Earley, P. 1992. *The Hot House: Life Inside Leavenworth Prison*. New York: Bantam Books.

Ehrenreich, R. M., C. L. Crumley, and J. E. Levy. 1995. *Heterarchy and the Analysis of Complex Societies*. American Anthropological Association Archaeological Paper No. 6. Arlington, Va.: American Anthropological Association.

Elia, R. J. 1991. "Conclusions and Recommendations." In Elia and Wesolowsky, *Archaeological Excavations*, 284–98.

Elia, R. J., and A. B. Wesolowsky, eds. 1991. *Archaeological Excavations at the Uxbridge Almshouse Burial Ground in Uxbridge, Massachusetts*. British Archaeological Reports International Series No. 564. Oxford: Tempus Reparatum.

Evans, R. 1982. *The Fabrication of Virtue*. Cambridge: Cambridge University Press.

Ezorsky, G. 1972. "The Ethics of Punishment." In *Philosophical Perspectives on Punishment*, edited by G. Ezorsky, xi-xxvii. Albany: State University of New York Press.

Farrell, M. M., and J. F. Burton. 2004. "Civil Rights and Moral Wrongs: World War II Japanese American Relocation Sites." *SAA Archaeological Record* 4(5): 22–25, 28.

Feinberg, J. 1972. "The Expressive Function of Punishment." In Ezorsky, *Philosophical Perspectives*, 25–34.

Feldman, A. 1991. *Formations of Violence: The Narrative of the Body and Political Terror in Northern Ireland*. Chicago: University of Chicago Press.

Ferrajoli, L., and D. Zolo. 1985. "Marxism and the Criminal Question." *Law and Philosophy* 4: 71–99.

Findlay, M., and R. Hogg. 1988. *Understanding Crime and Criminal Justice*. Sydney: Law Book Company.

Fisher-Giorlando, M. 1995. "Women in the Walls: The Imprisonment of Women at the Baton Rouge Penitentiary, 1835–1862." In Foster, Rideau, and Dennis, *The Wall is Strong*, 16–25.

Fleisher, M. S. 1989. *Warehousing Violence*. Newbury Park: Sage Publications.

———. 2001. "United States of America: The Federal System." In van Zyl Smit and Dünkel, *Imprisonment*, 676–94.

Foster, B. 1995. "Plantation Days at Angola: Major James and the Origins of Modern Corrections in Louisiana." In Foster, Rideau, and Dennis, *The Wall is Strong*, 1–5.

Foster, B., W. Rideau, and D. Dennis, eds. 1995. *The Wall Is Strong: Corrections in Louisiana*, 3rd ed. Lafayette: Center for Louisiana Studies, University of Southwestern Louisiana.

Foster, T. W. 1975. "Make-Believe Families: A Response of Women and Girls to the Deprivations of Imprisonment." *International Journal of Criminology and Penology* 3: 71–78.

Foucault, M. 1977. *Discipline and Punish*. Translated by A. Sheridan. New York: Vintage Books.

———. 1980. *The History of Sexuality*. Vol. 1, *An Introduction*. Translated by R. Hurley. New York: Vintage Books.

———. 2001 [1964]. *Madness and Civilization*. Translated by R. Howard. London: Routledge.

Fox, J. G. 1982. *Organizational and Racial Conflict in Maximum-Security Prisons*. Lexington, Mass.: Lexington Books.

Freedman, E. B. 1981. *Their Sisters' Keepers: Women's Prison Reform in America, 1830–1930*. Ann Arbor: University of Michigan Press.

Friedman, L. M. 1993. *Crime and Punishment in American History*. New York: Basic Books.

Gallo, E., and V. Ruggiero. 1991. "The Immaterial Prison: Custody as a Factory for the

Manufacture of Handicaps." *International Journal for the Sociology of Law* 19: 273–91.

Garland, D. 1983. "Philosophical Argument and Ideological Effect: An Essay Review." *Contemporary Crises* 7(1): 79–85.

———. 1990. *Punishment and Modern Society.* Oxford: Clarendon Press.

Garman, J. C. 1999. "'Detention Castles of Stone and Steel': A Historical Archaeology of the First Rhode Island State Prison, 1838–1878." Ph.D. diss., University of Massachusetts, Amherst.

———. 2005. *Detention Castles of Stone and Steel: Landscape, Labor, and the Urban Penitentiary.* Knoxville: University of Tennessee Press.

Garman, J. C., and P. A. Russo. 1999. "'A Disregard of Every Sentiment of Humanity': The Town Farm and Class Realignment in Nineteenth-century Rural New England." *Historical Archaeology* 33(1): 118–35.

Garofalo, J., and R. D. Clark. 1985. "The Inmate Subculture in Jails." *Criminal Justice and Behavior* 12(4): 415–34.

Gelsthorpe, L., and A. Morris. 1990. *Feminist Perspectives in Criminology.* Milton Keynes: Open University Press.

Gero, J. 2000. "Troubled Travels in Agency and Feminism." In *Agency in Archaeology,* edited by M. Dobres and J. E. Robb, 34–39. London: Routledge.

Giallombardo, R. 1966. *Society of Women: A Study of Women's Prisons.* New York: Wiley.

Gibb, J., and A. Beisaw. 2000. "Learning Cast Up from the Mire: Archaeological Investigations of Schoolhouses in the Northeastern United States." *Northeastern Historical Archaeology* 29: 107–29.

Giddens, A. 1979. *Central Problems in Social Theory: Action, Structure and Contradiction in Social Analysis.* Berkeley: University of California Press.

———. 1984. *The Constitution of Society: Outline of a Theory of Structuration.* Cambridge: Polity Press.

Gilchrist, R. 1994. *Gender and Material Culture: The Archaeology of Religious Women.* London: Routledge.

Glover, R. 2000. "Camp Ford from a Historical Perspective." In *Uncovering Camp Ford,* edited by A. V. Thoms, 27–37. Reports of Investigation, 1. College Station: Center for Ecological Archaeology, Texas A&M University.

Godelier, M. 1999. *The Enigma of the Gift.* Chicago: University of Chicago Press.

Goffman, E. 1961. *Asylums.* New York: Anchor Books.

Golden Gate National Parks Association (GGNPA). 1983. "Institutional Rules & Regulations: United States Penitentiary, Alcatraz, California." Unpublished document. San Francisco: National Parks Service.

Goldenberg, S., and D. Walsh. 2006. "Violent Clashes as Four Prisoners Try to Kill Themselves at Guantánamo Bay." *Guardian Newspaper.* May 20,2006.

Gramsci, A. 1971. *Selections from the Prison Notebooks.* Translated by Q. Hoare and G. Nowell Smith. New York: International Publishers.

Grauer, A. L., E. M. McNamara, and D. V. Houdek. 1998. "A History of Their Own: Patterns of Death in a Nineteenth-century Poorhouse." In Grauer and Stuart-Macadam, *Sex and Gender*, 149–64.

Grauer, A. L., and P. Stuart-Macadam, eds. 1998. *Sex and Gender in Paleopathological Perspective*. Cambridge: Cambridge University Press.

Gregory, C. A. 1982. *Gifts and Commodities*. London: Academic Press.

Haney, C. 1997. "'Infamous Punishment': The Psychological Consequences of Isolation." In Marquart and Sorensen, *Correctional Contexts*, 428–37.

Hartsock, N. 1990. "Foucault on Power: A Theory for Women?" In *Feminism/Postmodernism*, edited by L. J. Nicholson, 157–75. London: Routledge.

Hauff, J. L. 1988. "Wyoming's First Penitentiary: Archaeology of a Victorian Era Correctional Institution." *Wyoming Archaeologist* 31: 59–65.

Hazard, T. R. 1973 [1851]. *Report on the Poor and Insane in Rhode Island*. New York: Arno Press. Original housed in Rider Collection. John Hay Library, Brown University.

Heath, S. H. 1910. *Old English Houses of Alms*. London: Francis Griffiths.

Hebdige, D. 1988. *Hiding in the Light: On Images and Things*. London: Routledge.

Heffernan, E. 1972. *Making It in Prison*. New York: Wiley.

Hegel, G.W.F. 1969. *The Philosophy of Right*. Translated by T. M. Knox. London: Oxford University Press.

Henretta, J. 1973. *The Evolution of American Society, 1700–1815*. Lexington, Mass.: Heath.

Hertzberg, H. 1971. *The Search for an American Indian Identity: Modern Pan-Indian Movements*. New York: Syracuse University Press.

Hesseltine, W. B. 1930. *Civil War Prisons*. Columbus: Ohio State University Press.

Hirsch, A. J. 1992. *The Rise of the Penitentiary*. New Haven: Yale University Press.

Hobsbawm, E. 1973. "Peasants and Politics." *Journal of Peasant Studies* 1(1): 3–22.

Hornblum, A. M. 1998. *Acres of Skin: Human Experiments at Holmesburg Prison*. New York: Routledge.

Howard, J. 1784 [1777]. *The State of the Prisons in England and Wales*. London: Warrington.

Howe, A. 1994. *Punish and Critique: Towards a Feminist Analysis of Penality*. London: Routledge.

Huey, P. 2001. "The Almshouse in Dutch and English Colonial North America and its Precedent in the Old World: Historical and Archaeological Evidence." *International Journal of Historical Archaeology* 5(2): 123–54.

Ignatieff, M. 1978. *A Just Measure of Pain*. New York: Pantheon Books.

Inomata, T., and J. F. Burton. 1996. "World War II–Era Inscriptions." In Burton, *Three Farewells*, 659–84.

International Committee of the Red Cross (ICRC). 2005. "The Geneva Conventions: The Core of International Humanitarian Law." http://www.icrc.org/Web/Eng/siteeng0. nsf/html/genevaconventions (accessed February 20, 2007).

Irwin, J. 1980. *Prisons in Turmoil*. Boston: Little, Brown.

———. 1985. *The Jail: Managing the Underclass in American Society*. Berkeley: University of California Press.

———. 1990 [1970]. *The Felon*. 2nd ed. Berkeley: University of California Press.

Irwin, J., and J. Austin. 1994. *It's About Time: America's Imprisonment Binge*. Belmont: Wadsworth Publishing.

Jensen, G., and D. Jones. 1976. "Perspectives on Inmate Culture: A Study of Women in Prison." *Social Forces* 54(3): 590–603.

Johnson, M. 1999. "Rethinking Historical Archaeology." In *Historical Archaeology: Back From the Edge*, edited by P. Funari, M. Hall, and S. Jones, 23–36. London: Routledge.

Jones, R. S. 1993. "Coping with Separation: Adaptive Responses of Women Prisoners." *Women and Criminal Justice* 5(1): 71–97.

Kant, I. 1887. *The Philosophy of Law*. Part 2. Translated by W. Hastie. Edinburgh: T. T. Clark.

Katz, M. B. 1986. *In the Shadow of the Poorhouse*. New York: Basic Books.

Kent, S. 1999. "Egalitarianism, Equality, and Equitable Power." In Sweely, *Manifesting Power*, 30–48.

Kruttschnitt, C. 1981. "Prison Codes, Inmate Solidarity, and Women: A Reexamination." In *Comparing Female and Male Offenders*, edited by M. Q. Warren, 123–41. Beverly Hills: Sage Publications.

Kupers, T. 1999. *Prison Madness*. San Francisco: Jossey-Bass.

Landis, B. 1996. "About the Carlisle Indian Industrial School." *Modern American Poetry* http://www.english.uiuc.edu/maps/poets/a_f/erdrich/boarding/carlisle.htm (accessed May 12, 2004).

Lanphear, K. M. 1988. "Health and Mortality in a Nineteenth-century Poorhouse Skeletal Sample." Ph.D. diss., State University of New York, Albany.

Larson, L. H., and M. R. Crook. 1975. "An Archeological Investigation at Andersonville National Historic Site, Sumter and Macon Counties, Georgia." Unpublished report. Tallahassee: Southeast Archaeological Center, National Park Service.

Lévi-Strauss, C. 1987. Introduction to the Work of Marcel Mauss. London: Routledge and Kegan Paul.

Levy, J. E. 1999. "Gender, Power, and Heterarchy in Middle-level Societies." In Sweely, *Manifesting Power*, 62–78.

Levy, R. A. 2003. "Jose Padilla: No Charges and No Trial, Just Jail." *Chicago Sun-Times*, August 11, 2003. http://www.cato.org/dailys/08-21-03.html (accessed February 20, 2007).

Lewis, W. D. 1965. *From Newgate to Dannemora: The Rise of the Penitentiary in New York, 1796–1848*. Ithaca: Cornell University Press.

Liebling, A. 2000. "Prisoner Suicide and Prisoner Coping." In Tonry and Petersilia, *Prisons*, 283–361.

Liebling, A., and D. Price, 2001. *The Prison Officer*. London: Prison Service Journal.

Lindauer, O. 1996. *Historical Archaeology of the United States Industrial Indian School at Phoenix*. Anthropological Field Studies 42. Tempe: Arizona State University, Office of Cultural Resource Management.

———. 1997. *Not For School, But For Life*. Office of Cultural Resource Management Report 95. Tempe: Department of Anthropology, Arizona State University.

———. 1998. "Archaeology of the Phoenix Indian School." *Archaeology*, Online Features. http://www.archaeology.org/online/features/phoenix/ (accessed February 20, 2007).

Lindauer, O., and D. Ferguson. 1996. "Ceramic Artifacts." In Lindauer, *Historical Archaeology*, 141–57.

Linebaugh, P. 2003. *The London Hanged*. London: Verso.

Lomawaima, K. T. 1994. *They Called it Prairie Light: The Story of the Chilocco Indian School*. Lincoln: University of Nebraska Press.

Lombardo, L. X. 1989. *Guards Imprisoned: Correctional Officers at Work*. Cincinnati: Anderson Publishing Company.

Lovell, D., K. Cloyes, D. Allen, and L. Rhodes. 2000. "Who Lives in Supermaximum Custody? A Washington State Study." *Federal Probation* 64(2): 33–38.

Lucas, G. 1999. "The Archaeology of the Workhouse." In *The Familiar Past?*, edited by S. Tarlow and S. West, 125–39. London: Routledge.

Majewski, T. 1996. "Historical Ceramics." In Burton, *Three Farewells*, 793–862.

Markus, T. A. 1993. *Buildings and Power*. London: Routledge.

Marquardt, W. H. 1992. "Dialectical Archaeology." In *Archaeological Method and Theory*, vol. 4, edited by M. B. Schiffer, 101–40. Tucson: University of Arizona Press.

Marquart, J. W., and J. R. Sorensen, eds. 1997. *Correctional Contexts*. Los Angeles: Roxbury Publishing Company.

Marr, C. J. n.d. "Assimilation Through Education: Indian Boarding Schools in the Pacific Northwest." *Modern American Poetry* http://www.english.uiuc.edu/maps/poets/a_f/erdrich/boarding/marr.htm (accessed May 12, 2004).

Martin, S. J., and S. Ekland-Olson. 1987. *Texas Prisons: The Walls Came Tumbling Down*. Austin: Texas Monthly Press.

Martinson, R. 1972. "The Paradox of Prison Reform." In Ezorsky, *Philosophical Perspectives*, 309–27.

Mathiesen, T. 1990. *Prison on Trial: A Critical Assessment*. London: Sage Publications.

Mauss, M. 1990 [1950]. *The Gift*. New York: W.W. Norton.

McCartney, M. W. 1987. "Virginia's Workhouses for the Poor: Care for 'Divers Idle and Disorderly Persons.'" *North American Archaeologist* 8(4): 287–303.

McClintock, A. 1995. *Imperial Leather: Race, Gender and Sexuality in the Colonial Contest*. New York: Routledge.

McGowen, R. 1998. "The Well-Ordered Prison, England, 1780–1865." In Morris and Rothman, *Oxford History*, 71–99.

McKelvey, B. 1936. *American Prisons*. Chicago: University of Chicago Press.

McKenna, J. 1996. "Metal Artifacts." In Lindauer, *Historical Archaeology*, 159–69.

Melossi, D. 2000. "Changing Representations of the Criminal." *British Journal of Criminology* 40(2): 296–320.

Melossi, D., and M. Pavarini. 1981. *The Prison and the Factory: Origins of the Penitentiary System*. London: Macmillan.

Meskell, L. 1996. "The Somatization of Archaeology: Institutions, Discourses, Corporeality." *Norwegian Archaeological Review* 29(1): 1–16.

Miller, D., and C. Tilley. 1984. "Ideology, Power, and Prehistory: An Introduction." In

Ideology, Power, and Prehistory, edited by D. Miller and C. Tilley, 1–15. Cambridge: Cambridge University Press.

Miller, D., M. Rowlands, and C. Tilley. 1989. *Domination and Resistance*. London: Routledge.

Mohl, R. A. 1971. *Poverty in New York 1783–1825*. New York: Oxford University Press.

Moore, H. 1994. *A Passion for Difference: Essays in Anthropology and Gender*. Bloomington: Indiana University Press.

Morris, B. 1988. "Dhan-gadi Resistance to Assimilation." In *Being Black*, edited by I. Keen, 33–64. Canberra: Australian Institute of Aboriginal Studies.

Morris, N. 1998. "The Contemporary Prison, 1965–present." In Morris and Rothman, *Oxford History*, 202–31.

Morris, N., and D. J. Rothman, eds. 1998. *The Oxford History of the Prison*. Oxford: Oxford University Press.

Naffine, N. 1996. *Feminism and Criminality*. Philadelphia: Temple University Press.

Nash, R. 1996. "Manzanar from the Inside." In Burton, *Three Farewells*, 109–22.

National Park Service. 1993. "Alcatraz Development Concept Plan and Environmental Assessment." Unpublished report prepared by LSA Associates, Inc., Point Richmond, California, for the Golden Gate National Recreation Area, National Park Service, San Francisco.

Nelson, S. M. 1997. *Gender in Archaeology: Analyzing Power and Prestige*. Walnut Creek: AltaMira Press.

Nettels, C. P. 1962. *The Emergence of a National Economy, 1775–1815*. New York: Holt, Rinehart and Winston.

Nobles, C. H. 2000. "Gazing upon the Invisible: Women and Children at the Old Baton Rouge Penitentiary." *American Antiquity* 65(1): 5–14.

Novak, D. A. 1978. *The Wheel of Servitude: Black Forced Labor After Slavery*. Lexington: University Press of Kentucky.

Odier, P. 1982. *Alcatraz. The Rock: A History of Alcatraz: The Fort/The Prison*. Eagle Rock: L'Image Odier Publishing Company.

O'Donovan, M. 2002. *The Dynamics of Power*. Center for Archaeological Investigation, Occasional Paper No. 30. Carbondale: Southern Illinois University.

Owen, B. 1998. *In the Mix: Struggle and Survival in a Women's Prison*. New York: State University of New York Press.

Parenti, C. 1999. *Lockdown America: Police and Prisons in the Age of Crisis*. London: Verso.

Peña, E. S. 1992. "Educational Archaeology: Historical Archaeological Investigations at Schoolhouse 12 in the Town of LeRay, Jefferson County." *Journal of the New York State Archaeological Association* 103: 10–19.

———. 2001. "The Role of Wampum Production at the Albany Almshouse." *International Journal of Historical Archaeology* 5(2): 155–74.

Piddock, S. 2001. "'An Irregular and Inconvenient Pile of Buildings': The Destitute Asylum of Adelaide, South Australia and the English Workhouse." *International Journal of Historical Archaeology* 5(1): 73–95.

Ponsford, M. 1994. "Post-medieval Britain and Ireland in 1993." *Post-Medieval Archaeology* 28: 119–83.

Pratt, J. 2002. *Punishment and Civilization*. London: Sage Publications.

Prendergast, M., J. Wellisch, and G. Falkin. 1995. "Assessment of and Services for Substance-Abusing Women Offenders in Community and Correctional Settings." *The Prison Journal* 75(2): 240–56.

Prentice, G., and M. C. Prentice. 2000. "Far from the Battlefield: Archaeology at Anderson Prison." In *Archaeological Perspectives on the American Civil War*, edited by C. R. Geier and S. R. Potter, 166–87. Gainesville: University Press of Florida.

Preston, M. 1992. "A Preliminary Report on the Historical Archaeology at the Patapsco Female Institute (18HO143), Ellicott City, Maryland." *Maryland Archaeology* 28(1): 14–32.

Prout, C., and R. Ross. 1988. *Care and Punishment: The Dilemmas of Prison Medicine*. Pittsburgh: University of Pittsburgh Press.

Rafter, N. H. 1985. *Partial Justice: Women in State Prisons, 1800–1935*. Boston: Northeastern University Press.

———. 1990. *Partial Justice: Women, Prisons and Social Control*. 2nd ed. New Brunswick: Transaction Publishers.

Rhodes, L. A. 2001. "Toward an Anthropology of Prisons." *Annual Review of Anthropology* 30: 65–83.

Rideau, W. 1995. "The Clubs." In Foster, Rideau, and Dennis, *The Wall is Strong*, 107–10.

Roberts, C. A., M. E. Lewis, and P. Boocock. 1998. "Infectious Disease, Sex, and Gender: The Complexity of It All." In Grauer and Stuart-Macadam, *Sex and Gender*, 93–113.

Ross, S. 1988. "Objects of Charity: Poor Relief, Poverty, and the Rise of the Almshouse in Early Eighteenth-century New York City." In *Authority and Resistance in Early New York*, edited by W. Pencak and C. E. Wright, 138–72. New York: New York Historical Society.

Rothman, D. 1990. *The Discovery of the Asylum*. 2nd ed. Boston: Little, Brown and Company.

Rusche, G. 1978. "Labour Market and Penal Sanction: Thoughts on the Sociology of Criminal Justice." *Crime and Social Justice* 10: 2–8.

Rusche, G., and O. Kirchheimer. 1968. *Punishment and Social Structure*. New York: Russell and Russell.

Russell, M. 2004. "Prison Numbers Increase to Nearly 1.5 Million Despite Decade-long Drop in Crime." Press release. Justice Policy Institute Newsroom (online). http://www.justicepolicy.org/article.php?id=462 (accessed February 20, 2007).

Schama, S. 1987. *The Embarrassment of Riches: An Interpretation of Dutch Culture in the Golden Age*. New York: Alfred A. Knopf.

Schiraldi, V. 2002. "Spend More Money on Education, Not Prisons." Justice Policy Institute Newsroom (online). http://www.justicepolicy.org/article.php?id=94 (accessed February 20, 2007).

Schneider, D. M. 1938. *The History of Public Welfare in New York State*. Chicago: University of Chicago Press.

Scott, J. C. 1985. *Weapons of the Weak: Everyday Forms of Peasant Resistance*. New Haven: Yale University Press.

———. 1990. *Domination and the Arts of Resistance: Hidden Transcripts*. New Haven: Yale University Press.

Semple, J. 1993. *Bentham's Prison*. Oxford: Clarendon Press.

Snyder, S. L., and D. T. Mitchell. 2001. "Re-engaging the Body: Disability Studies and the Resistance to Embodiment." *Public Culture* 13(3): 367–89.

South, S. 1977. *Method and Theory in Historical Archaeology*. New York: Academic Press.

Spencer-Wood, S. M. 1996. "Feminist Historical Archaeology and Domestic Reform." In *Historical Archaeology and the Study of American Culture*, edited by L. De Cunzo and B. Herman, 397–446. Winterthur, Del.: Winterthur Museum.

———. 1999. "Gendering Power." In Sweely, *Manifesting Power*, 175–83.

Spencer-Wood, S. M., and S. Baugher. 2001. "Introduction and Historical Context for the Archaeology of Institutions of Reform. Part I: Asylums." *International Journal of Historical Archaeology* 5(1): 3–17.

Spierenburg, P. 1998. "The Body and the State: Early Modern Europe." In Morris and Rothman, *Oxford History*, 44–70.

Spitzer, S. 1979. "Notes Toward a Theory of Punishment and Social Change." *Research in Law and Sociology* 2: 207–29.

Stallybrass, P., and A. White. 1986. *The Politics and Poetics of Transgression*. London: Methuen.

Stanton, A. H., and M. S. Schwartz. 1954. *The Mental Hospital*. New York: Basic Books.

Starr, F. 2001. "Convict Artefacts from the Civil Hospital Privy on Norfolk Island." *Australasian Historical Archaeology* 19: 39–47.

Stoler, A. L. 1995. *Race and the Education of Desire*. Durham: Duke University Press.

Strathern, M. 1988. *The Gender of the Gift*. Berkeley: University of California Press.

Strauss, A. E., and S. Spencer-Wood. 1999. "Phase II Archaeological Site Examination at the Artist's Guild/Old Poor House Building in Falmouth, Massachusetts." Unpublished report prepared by Cultural Resource Specialists of New England for the Town of Falmouth.

Sweely, T. L., ed. *Manifesting Power*. London: Routledge.

Sykes, G. M. 1958. *The Society of Captives*. New York: Rinehart.

Sykes, G. M., and S. L. Messinger. 1960. "The Inmate Social System." In *Theoretical Studies in Social Organization of the Prison*, edited by R. Cloward, 6–10. New York: Social Science Research Council.

Takagi, P. 1993. "The Walnut Street Jail: A Penal Reform to Centralize the Powers of the State." In *Crime and Capitalism*, edited by E. F. Greenberg, 533–45. Philadelphia: Temple University Press.

Tarlow, S. 2002. "Excavating Utopia: Why Archaeologists Should Study 'Ideal' Communities of the Nineteenth Century." *International Journal of Historical Archaeology* 6(4): 299–323.

Teeters, N. K., and J. D. Shearer. 1957. *The Prison at Philadelphia, Cherry Hill: The Separate System of Prison Discipline, 1829–1913*. New York: Columbia University Press.

Thomas, Jim. 1993. *Doing Critical Ethnography*. Newbury Park: Sage Publications.

Thomas, Julian. 2002. "Taking Power Seriously." In O'Donovan, *Dynamics of Power*, 35–50.

Thompson, E. N. 1979. "The Rock: A History of Alcatraz Island, 1847–1972: Historic Resource Study." Unpublished report for the Historic Preservation Division, National Park Service, Denver.

Thoms, A. V. 2004. "Sand Blows Desperately: Land-Use History and Site Integrity at Camp Ford, a Confederate POW Camp in East Texas." *Historical Archaeology* 38(4): 73–95.

Tittle, C. R., and D. P. Tittle. 1964. "Social Organization of Prisoners." *Social Forces* 43(2): 216–21.

Toch, H. 1977. *Living in Prison: The Ecology of Survival*. New York: Free Press.

Tomlinson, H. 1980. "Design and Reform: The 'Separate System' in the Nineteenth-century English Prison." In *Buildings and Society*, edited by A. D. King, 94–119. London: Routledge and Kegan Paul.

Tonry, M., and J. Petersilia, eds. 2000. *Prisons*. Chicago: University of Chicago Press.

Trennert, R. A. 1988. *The Phoenix Indian School: Forced Assimilation in Arizona, 1891–1935*. Norman: University of Oklahoma Press.

Trigger, D. 1992. *Whitefella Comin': Aboriginal Responses to Colonialism in Northern Australia*. Cambridge: Cambridge University Press.

Trocolli, R. 1999. "Women Leaders in Native North American Societies: Invisible Women of Power." In Sweely, *Manifesting Power*, 49–61.

Turner, V. 1969. *The Ritual Process: Structure and Anti-Structure*. Chicago: Aldine.

Upton, D. 1992. "The City as Material Culture." In *The Art and Mystery of Historical Archaeology*, edited by A. Yentsch and M. C. Beaudry, 51–72. Boca Raton: CRC Press.

U.S. Department of Defense (DoD). 2002. "Secretary Rumsfeld Media Availability en route to Guantanamo Bay, Cuba." News Transcript (online). http://www.defenselink.mil/transcripts/2002/t01282002_t0127enr.html (accessed February 20, 2007).

Uyeda, C. I. 1995. *Due Process: Americans of Japanese Ancestry and the United States Constitution*. San Francisco: National Japanese American Historical Society.

van Zyl Smit, D., and F. Dünkel, eds. 2001. *Imprisonment Today and Tomorrow*. 2nd ed. The Hague: Kluwer Law International.

Wacquant, L. 2001. "Deadly Symbiosis: When Ghetto and Prison Meet and Mesh." In *Mass Imprisonment: Social Causes and Consequences*, edited by D. Garland, 82–120. London: Sage Publications.

Wall, D. D. 1994. *The Archaeology of Gender: Separating the Spheres in Urban America*. New York: Plenum Press.

Walmsley, R. 2001. "World Prison Populations: An Attempt at a Complete List." In van Zyl Smit and Dünkel, *Imprisonment*, 775–95.

Ward, D. A., and G. G. Kassebaum. 1965. *Women's Prison: Sex and Social Structure*. Chicago: Aldine.

Weber, M. 1947. *The Theory of Social and Economic Organization*. Oxford: Oxford University Press.

Weiner, A. 1992. *Inalienable Possessions*. Berkeley: University of California Press.

Wesolowsky, A. B. 1991. "The Osteology of the Uxbridge Paupers." In Elia and Wesolowsky, *Archaeological Excavations*, 230–53.

Wilde, O. 1999 [1905]. *De profundis*. Ware: Wordsworth Editions.

Williams, R. 1977. *Marxism and Literature*. Oxford: Oxford University Press.

Williams, L., and K. Flinn. 1990. *Trade Wampum: New Jersey to the Plains*. Trenton: New Jersey State Museum.

Williams, V. L., and M. Fish. 1974. *Convicts, Codes, and Contraband: The Prison Life of Men and Women*. Cambridge: Ballinger.

Wilson, T. W. 1986. "Gender Differences in the Inmate Code." *Canadian Journal of Criminology* 28(4): 397–405.

Wolf, E. R. 1990. "Distinguished Lecture: Facing Power—Old Insights, New Questions." *American Anthropologist* 92: 586–96.

Wurtzburg, S., and T. H. Hahn. 1992a. "Hard Labor: A Cultural Resources Survey of the Old Louisiana State Penitentiary, Baton Rouge, Louisiana." Unpublished report by Coastal Environments Ltd., Baton Rouge.

———. 1992b *Hard Labor: History and Archaeology at the Old Louisiana State Penitentiary, Baton Rouge, Louisiana*. Fort Worth: General Services Administration.

Zedner, L. 1991. *Women, Crime and Custody in Victorian England*. Oxford: Clarendon Press.

Zingraff, M., and R. Zingraff. 1980. "Adaptation Patterns of Incarcerated Female Delinquents." *Juvenile and Family Court Journal* 31(2): 35–47.

Index

Eleanor Conlin Casella is a senior lecturer in archaeology at the University of Manchester, United Kingdom. She is the author of *Archaeology of the Ross Female Factory* (2002) and coeditor of *The Archaeology of Plural and Changing Identities* (2005) and *Industrial Archaeology: Future Directions* (2005). She has directed fieldwork projects in Australia, Europe, and the United States.